COVERED

Living In Triumph While Going Through Trials

By

JACKIE DIGHANS

Covered: Living in Triumph While Going Through Trials
Publisher of Peace
Miles City, Montana
Copyright ©2022 by Jackie Dighans. All rights reserved.

Scripture quotations, unless otherwise noted, are taken from the Amplified® Bible (AMP), Copyright © 2015 by The Lockman Foundation. Used by permission. www.lockman.org.

Scripture quotations marked NIV are taken from THE HOLY BIBLE, NEW INTERNATIONAL VERSION®, NIV® Copyright © 1973, 1978, 1984, 2011 by Biblica, Inc.® Used by permission. All rights reserved worldwide.

Scripture quotations marked NLT are taken from the *Holy Bible*, New Living Translation, copyright © 1996, 2004, 2015 by Tyndale House Foundation. Used by permission of Tyndale House Publishers, Inc., Carol Stream, Illinois 60188. All rights reserved.

Scripture quotations marked NKJV are taken from the New King James Version®. Copyright © 1982 by Thomas Nelson. Used by permission. All rights reserved.

ISBN: 978-0-578-26878-1
Library of Congress Control Number: 2022912615
Cover and interior design by: worldlight_gfx/fiverr
Editing by: Words With Jas LLC
Illustrations by: Rayne Idland Photography and Photos by Kristy
All rights reserved by Jackie Dighans and Publisher of Peace.
Printed in the United States of America.

TABLE OF CONTENTS

This book is dedicated to my husband, Justin, and my children (Jayna, Summer, Luke, Logen, Alena, Easton, Jaclyn, Lindy, Blaize, and Evangelia), who have been so patient with me as I continue to learn so many things as a wife, mom, entrepreneur, and now author. To my first paid coach, who helped get this book, that was already inside me, started. To a few of my coach friends, who gave great feedback on the first draft of my book and helped me self-publish. But first and foremost, to my Heavenly Father, who is with me, guiding me every step of the way.

Thank you.

INTRODUCTION

What if our past, if we hold the right mindset around it, can propel us to the prize of the high call of God? What if all the circumstances we are walking through are preparing us for God's purpose for us? What if the way we go through life is the most important lesson? What are we allowing to be produced in us as we walk through circumstances?

The Word says in James 1:2–4, "Consider it pure joy, my brothers and sisters, whenever you face trials of many kinds, because you know that the testing of your faith produces perseverance. Let perseverance finish its work so that you may be mature and complete, not lacking anything."

What if we decide to do what this Word advises? What could our lives look like if we consider it a joy, even pure joy, when trials come? Is that unimaginable? Hold on, though, look what it says. Because you KNOW that the testing of your faith produces … Let's stop right there. What are you going to let your trials produce in you as a child of God? You don't have to let the trials produce negative thoughts and ways in you; the trials can move you forward. All of us go through trials. Why not decide you won't let them move you or shake you? Why not let them do their work in you and make you mature and complete, lacking nothing?

This book is about the circumstances in my life and how I didn't just simply overcome the trials. My trials include my parents' divorce, my dad being killed in a car accident, moving to a new state in high school, and attending three high schools in four years. My trials include my sister and brother-in-law dying of cancer within four years of each other and leaving three kids behind. My trials include dealing with people who are intrusive, helping to support my husband during his season of breakdown and depression, and switching seven kids from home school to public school—a total lifestyle change. My trials include my husband being gone more than he was home for a year and a half, and me going back to school in my forties as a mom of ten children.

I kept a perspective of "What can I learn through these trials?" I didn't want to go through the same trial in the same way again. Did you hear that? I didn't want to go through the same trial in the same way again. That meant that I would have to be intentional about how I go through life. If I had to go through it again, I wanted to do it stronger and with a different mindset that would make it easier the next time.

How about you? How do you want to go through hard times? This book will help you see that you do have a choice. It all depends on the result you want: growth and maturity, or stuck and lukewarm. Thank you in advance for walking through my life story with me. I came out the other side facing my trials triumphantly, and I believe you will face your trials triumphantly too.

The reason I chose to title this book *Covered* is that I can see that I am where I am today because my Lord and Savior has covered me all throughout my life. He has protected, provided, healed, shielded, and sheltered me in every way. I am eternally grateful for all He has done in and through me. I want to give Him glory and share His story of my life to the world.

Love you, friend,

Jackie Dighans

CHAPTER 1

I Thought We Didn't Believe in That ...

It started out a normal day when I was an early-elementary-age girl, seven or eight years old. Suddenly, everything changed.

First let me describe my life before that day. I was the middle daughter; one sister was three years older than me, and the other was one year younger. I enjoyed playing house with my younger sister, and we played kickball in the yard with our neighbors. I would walk down the alley to get to school. And I always remember dinner as a family around the table. Some nights there was a Bible story at bedtime, and my favorite was the story of Moses. The picture I remember most was when he was floating in a basket in the water. Pharaoh's daughter and maidservants were on the edge of the river, pointing at the infant in the basket among the reeds.

I'm writing this book and picturing myself as an adult, with all the things God has been doing in my life, and I'm in that place of floating on the water of my life, in God's hands, just like Moses.

When I was a child, our family was part of a small Baptist church in our rural Montana community, and we went to Sunday school regularly. My dad taught an adult Sunday school class, and my mom served with the women's group in the church. We participated in caroling and the Christmas plays, and every year, our family attended the New Year's Eve party in the Parsonage right there at the church. These were some of the activities I remember looking forward to and enjoying as a child.

During my early years, my parents owned an antique store called J&A Antiques. The J and A stood for the first initials of their names. We enjoyed going to flea markets, antique stores, and estate sales, and we collected antiques as a family. My sisters and I each chose something to collect so that when we went to these different sales, we could look for our own antique collectible. My older sister collected bells, my younger sister collected dolls, and I chose miniatures. I thought those small, ornate mini things were so cute. It was an activity we did as a family, and I enjoyed that time.

Our antique store was in an old building on Main Street in our town. I remember going to our store after school or after swimming and smelling the scent of furniture being refinished and seeing the dust in the air from the sander. The upstairs in this building was an amazing spot for my sisters and me. It had a wide-open space where we could roller skate. Under the floorboards, we would find treasures like old bottles and pop cans from a business that had been there years before.

My family was important to me, and I enjoyed our time together. I'm not even sure how long we owned this antique store, but in my child's mind, it was a huge part of my life. The important thing was that we did it as a family.

It's interesting that what we remember from childhood wasn't necessarily something we did all the time. We may have only done it two or three times, and maybe for just a short season, but it impacts a child's life immensely.

I remember our summer vacation to California. My dad was in the Army Reserve, and we spent several weeks in our camper on the base while he was training one summer. There were a bunch of boarded up and abandoned old buildings on the base called barracks. One of the barracks was open for the families that were camping so we could use its bathroom facilities.

A few other families were camping in the same area; their dads were doing the same thing my dad was doing. On my dad's days off, we would go sightseeing. I loved the ocean then and still do to this day: the waves crashing, the cool brisk mist on my face. And oh, the seashells we would collect. At that time, we even collected starfish. We dried them out in the sun on the ground next to our camper. It was fun bringing a bit of the ocean back to our home in Montana.

One beach we visited was covered with elephant seals. It was like walking through a maze among these humongous seals. I remember my dad even pulled on the tail of one of these massive animals. It lifted its head and let out a roar. My mom was not happy, but I loved the adventure. This was obviously before the beach was regulated. I visited this same beach with my husband and children several years ago, and we could only see the seals with binoculars from quite a distance because of regulations that had been put in place. It was a bit of a disappointment but fun to go back to that area as an adult with my own family. This summer vacation I took as a kid seemed like it was such a huge part of my growing up, even though it was only one summer. It was one of the last things we did as a family.

But back to that day when my world completely changed. Daddy was moving out. My parents were separating, and I heard the word "divorce." My first thought at eight years old was, "I thought we didn't believe in that." I must have heard in church, school, or from my parents that divorce was not good. I must have had the idea that divorce was not an option for my parents; after all, they loved each other. At least I thought they did. My foundation was shaken, and it felt like it was crumbling. All I had known was slipping out from under me. That is how I felt.

I liked going to church as a family. I liked evening meals as a family. I liked going to the antique store while my parents were working and roller skating in the empty rooms above, skating round and round with my sisters. I liked going to the flea markets to find miniatures for my collection and helping my sisters find their bells or dolls for their collections. I didn't want any of that to end.

I realized I had no say in this decision. My dad moved out of the house and into the apartment above the antique store. My insecurities began to rise. I was already described as a shy, quiet little girl, and after this trauma, my younger sister and I were often asked, "Do you talk?"

My sisters and I were staying with him one weekend when it was "his turn" to have us. We witnessed my dad struggling with alcohol. He was drunk. We had never seen him like that before. We were all in bed in the same room, and we heard him staggering down the long hallway in the apartment. His boots were clomping loudly on the hardwood floor as he went. I remember lying in bed, scared and listening. We heard yelling, cussing, and angry arguing. He was on the phone with my mom and then with other friends or relatives. He was crying. He didn't like what was happening, but he obviously didn't know how to change it. The crying and angry conversations on the phone went on for what seemed like hours, and then I heard him clomp back down the hall. The door slammed shut, and he was gone again. He wasn't trying to hurt us. My sisters and I were safe, but the horror of the night lingered on. What would happen next? When would this terrifying night end?

Finally, it was morning. My dad had not returned to the apartment. My sisters and I got up and made bowls of cereal and waited for our mom to come pick us up, uncertain of what would happen from that point on. Upon her arrival, we learned that my dad had been in a motorcycle accident that night. He was scraped up but okay, only by the grace of God. Hurriedly, we packed up our things, anxious about what we had experienced the night before. I don't recall ever going back to that apartment unless it was to get a few more things. At that point, my parents' antique store was closed. My dad ended up leaving town. He may have gone to Michigan to visit his family for a while, and then he came back to pack up his things.

I don't know how long he had been gone; it may have been just a few weeks. The next time I remember seeing him was Christmastime. I remember passing him as we were being driven back to school after lunch. He was in his Jeep, the kind that has the option of taking off the top and sides. Of course, it was all put together at this time because it was the middle of winter in Montana. I wanted to stop him and say hi and give him a big hug, but we had to get back to school. We didn't see him until that evening or the next day. I don't even know for sure what we did during that time with him. We probably ate dinner together that evening and visited with him for a bit.

He informed us that he was moving to Daytona Beach, Florida, where he had a friend. He would be able to work on building a deck on some beach property. Right away, we voiced how sad we would be to see him go and said we wanted to come live with him for the summer as soon as school was out. That was our plan. The next few months left my sisters and me dreaming of summer with our dad at the beach in Florida.

Our mom, meanwhile, had remarried and given birth to a baby, so we had a new half-brother. From the outside, my mom stayed very steady and stable during the separation and then divorce. I know it wasn't easy for her as a single mom for a season. She started working in a city office in our town and stayed very consistent at home. She was a good mom. I see her as a pillar. Standing through all the ups and downs of life. I am very thankful for who she has been in my life.

What surprises came up for you as a child? Did anything catch you off guard? Is there anything you need to settle with? Circumstances that we go through as children can limit us in life if we don't look at our thoughts around them and settle them with God, ourselves, and others.

> *The Bible says in Philippians 3:13–14: "Brothers and sisters, I do not consider that I have made it my own yet; but one thing I do: forgetting what lies behind and reaching forward to what lies ahead, I press on toward the goal to win the [heavenly] prize of the upward call of God in Christ Jesus."*

Imagine forgetting or leaving the past behind. What would that look like in your life? What do you need to stop dragging along with you from the past? Settling with it will set you free to reach toward what lies ahead.

YOUR NEXT STEPS JOURNALING

_____

_____

_____

_____

_____

_____

_____

_____

_____

_____

_____

_____

_____

_____

_____

_____

_____

_____

_____

_____

_____

_____

CHAPTER 2

DADDY DIED

A t this point, I realized that I could carry the baggage of what happened throughout my whole life. Or I could drop off the bags and let the trials make me stronger.

I still vividly remember the day. I had ridden my bike to school that morning. I was twelve years old and in the seventh grade. I always met a friend at the corner a couple of blocks down the street from my house, and we would ride our bikes together to school. This day was the same. I had a normal day at school and was looking forward to track practice after school. I was about half a block from my house, and my friend and I had already parted ways. It was unusual for me to see my mom's car coming toward me at that time in the afternoon. She should have been at work.

As the car got closer, I could see that my sister Laurie was driving. She was just a few years older than me. Questions quickly came to my mind. *Why isn't my mom at work? Why is my sister driving my mom's car toward me?* It didn't make sense, but I would soon find out. As Laurie approached, I could see that she had been crying. She mouthed the words "Daddy died." Right away, I said, "What did you say?" as if I didn't hear her or understand her the first time. I think I said that because I didn't want to hear or believe what she had just told me. I wanted to believe I had misunderstood or didn't hear her.

I continued riding my bike the short distance home, and she continued down the street in the opposite direction. The rest of my ride home was different after that. I was shaking and saying "No, no, no!" I parked my bike in its normal spot on the side of our house. As I attempted to lock my bike to the railing, I was shaking too hard and tears were building up, and I almost couldn't get it locked. Finally, I got it and went inside. Upon entering, I knew what Laurie had said was true. I did hear her right. Our pastor was there, and my mom was home from work. I was greeted with red eyes and somber looks. Another family friend or two were also there. They all wanted to hug me, but I didn't want to be hugged or even touched.

The phone rang, and my Uncle Doug (my dad's middle sister's husband) from Michigan was calling, wanting to talk to me and tell me what had happened. I put the phone up to my ear. He proceeded to tell me that my dad had been in a car accident in Florida the day before. It was raining, and the road was wet. A friend of his was driving my dad's Jeep with the top and sides off. On the slippery road, he lost control of the vehicle. The Jeep rolled, causing my dad to be thrown from it. He landed on some rocks on the side of the road, and he died instantly from internal bleeding.

I couldn't believe what I was hearing. *My dad was gone. Could this be true?* I had been planning to go live with him for the summer. It was April 16, and we only had another month and a half left before we would be able to see him again. *Why did this happen?*

I wanted to run away. I wanted to be alone. I left the house and headed to track practice. It was my first year of this sport in junior high, and I had only practiced a time or two before. At practice, still in shock from the news, I told my coach what had happened. I didn't want to be home, but I also didn't feel like practicing with the team. I didn't know where I wanted to be; I didn't feel like I belonged anywhere at that moment.

The next thing I knew, my mom, my sisters, and I were flying to Michigan for the funeral. That is where Daddy grew up and his family still lived. He would be buried near his dad, who, coincidentally, had been killed by a tree falling on him when my dad was twelve.

At the funeral, I remember hearing my relatives talking about how my dad didn't look natural and his hair wasn't fixed right. I wondered how much better a dead man in a coffin could look. *Why does that even matter?* The thing that mattered to me was I no longer had a living dad, and how would life look now? We enjoyed our time with the Michigan family for a couple of weeks and then came back to reality.

Everything had changed so much in the last year. At that time, I didn't see my stepdad as my dad. My half-brother, the new baby in the house, was adorable, but I didn't know how much I wanted to love him. But how could I not love this chunky, cute baby boy? I didn't want to get attached; I was mad. Mad about the divorce. Mad about my mom remarrying. Mad about her having a baby. Mad about my dad moving. And now mad about him dying. Things weren't going right for me, but I couldn't do anything about any of it. I couldn't change the circumstances, but I could decide how I would come through it all.

I was feeling empty, and I tried drinking alcohol. I also tried relationships with guys. It was fun for a season but not fulfilling. Nothing could fill the emptiness.

At one point, my dad had given me a devotional. It was called *If God Loves Me, Why Can't I Get My Locker Open?* I began to read that book regularly. I would look up the scriptures and journal my thoughts and prayers.

A couple of years later, we moved to Idaho where my stepdad had accepted a new job. I didn't know anyone there, and it would mean a new start for me. New school, new friends, new house, new life. I thought I would like it, but the first year was a struggle. I was just starting my sophomore year of high school in a school three times the size of the one I came from. It wasn't easy meeting new people. I wasn't terribly outgoing. I wanted to go back to our small town in Montana because I missed the familiar. I had thought I wanted this move, but it was hard on me.

I had experienced enough "hard" by the time I was sixteen years old. At times, I would ponder the difficulties I had faced in childhood, and I realized that at that age, we have so much life ahead of us. If we quit being willing to do hard things at a young age, how will we do the rest of our lives? At that point, I started a journey to figure out how to go through hard stuff and use it to make me stronger. My younger sister and I joined a youth group that was part of our family's new church.

> *Like it says in James 1:2–3, "Consider it nothing but joy, my brothers and sisters, whenever you fall into various trials. Be assured that the testing of your faith [through experience] produces endurance [leading to spiritual maturity, and inner peace]."*

Through this move and the youth group, I rededicated my life to the Lord. I was at a winter retreat, and I asked Jesus to be my Savior and the Lord of my life. I had been baptized and prayed the salvation prayer in my early elementary years before my parents' divorce, but a lot had happened since then. I felt I needed a new start in my spiritual life. On my bunk, in the lodge, I renewed my commitment to the Lord. I knew my life would never be the same after that night.

Up to this point, I had attended public schools. The following year, I switched to a private school for my last two years of high school. These years were good, but during that time at this private school, I realized how I *didn't* want to be as a Christian. Many of the kids did exactly what the rest of the world did, and I was in that group. However, I knew that moving forward, I wanted something different, and I wanted to be different and look different as a believer.

Because of the life experiences I had walked through in my youth—my parents' divorce, my mom getting remarried and having a baby, my dad getting killed in a car accident, and moving to a town where I didn't know anyone in high school—I wanted to help other people get through hard things. Since my dad's death, I desired to be a Christian counselor.

Right after my last year of high school, I went to a Bible college in Portland, Oregon, for one year. At one of the conferences held at the school, I committed my life to serving the Lord. I was, at that point, willing to go wherever He wanted me to go. I thought I would be called to be a missionary overseas. At that time, becoming a missionary was a common path for people who felt called to serve. At least that was what I had observed in the circles I was in. I liked to travel, and I had been to Mexico on a summer mission trip with my youth group and to Bermuda with a friend for a work trip with her dad. To me, traveling was interesting and adventurous. I did not know what my life would look like, but I was willing and open to what God would call me to do.

My first specific opportunity to serve the Lord after I made that commitment was a summer-long mission trip to Macau, a city located on the southern tip of China. I went with a team from my Bible college, plus others from a church in California, to share the gospel while teaching English in the churches. Before I decided to go, the Lord gave me this verse:

> *"O taste and see that the Lord [our God] is good; How blessed [fortunate, prosperous, and favored by God] is the man who takes refuge in Him." Psalm 34:8*

I felt like He was saying, "Step out, do the next thing, get a taste of serving me and doing the unfamiliar thing, and you will see that I am good. If you don't step out and do this next thing, you won't get a taste of My goodness. So,

I did; I signed up. I wrote the support letters, and I got the required shots. The next thing I knew, I was on the plane to Hong Kong and then on to Macau by ferry. I was by myself, with people I didn't know well, doing something I had never done before. It was an amazing summer. I'm so glad I listened to what the Lord was saying: "Just take a step, taste and see that I am good and that obeying Me is good." I heard once that in some countries, the people move their mouths in a way that they are tasting His goodness when they hear the gospel.

Have you tasted His goodness? What is God calling you to step out into? He wants to show you His goodness, one taste at a time.

During my last years of high school and my first year of college, I pushed myself to get past the trauma of what had happened with my parents' divorce, my dad's death, the move, etc. I didn't want those situations to shape me in a negative way. I wanted to grow stronger through them and help other people in their distress. I can see now how God led me through this path of life so I could help people on a higher level. For many years, I didn't even think about becoming a counselor. Life is like an onion with so many layers of thoughts about the circumstances we go through. We can lose sight of our dreams, thinking they will never happen. But we serve a God of the impossible. He brought me full circle after having ten kids, with three of them now married. I have seven children left in the house.

Remember I said I wanted to become a Christian counselor? Well, over twenty years later, I am now a Covenant Life Coach, coaching people to get in alignment with the Covenant of God so they can live their lives in the fullness and abundance that God has planned for us.

Have you lost sight of your dreams? Have the circumstances of life left you wondering why you're here and what your purpose is? You are here for a reason. You may need someone who can help you leave your past behind and throw off the weights and sins that so easily entangle you. You can feel free to run your race and reach the goal of the high call of God. He has more for you than you could ask for or imagine. Taste and see.

MOVING FORWARD JOURNALING

_____

_____

_____

_____

_____

_____

_____

_____

_____

_____

_____

_____

_____

_____

_____

_____

_____

_____

_____

_____

_____

_____

_____

_____

_____

CHAPTER 3

CAN I TRUST YOU?

What do you do when you find out someone isn't who you thought they were? And what about if that someone is your spouse?

My husband and I started dating in our junior year of high school. We had one of those long-distance relationships because he was in Montana, and I had moved to Idaho. We had met right before I moved away, just after our freshman year. A couple of people were acquainted with both of us and kept us caught up on what each other was doing.

The summer after I moved to Idaho, my sister got married back in my hometown in Montana, and I was her maid of honor. This wedding brought me back to my old stomping grounds for a few weeks. I ended up meeting up with Justin, now my husband, while I was out with some friends one evening. He brought me to the home I was staying in while I was there for the wedding. I invited him to the wedding, and that began our long-distance relationship that would last on and off for four years. The distance, as well as our own insecurities and baggage from the past, caused some breakups along the way.

We ended up getting married in the fourth year of our relationship. During our dating years, I had access to standby airplane tickets since my stepdad was employed with Horizon/Alaskan Air. I would hop on the plane for several visits, one of them being prom our senior year.

We both graduated from high school the same year. Justin attended a college in Montana a couple hours from his hometown, and I was led to go to a Bible college in the Portland, Oregon, area. For me, it was a year of growth, seeking God and His will for my life. Justin's focus that year was college football and all that goes along with it. Again, we would visit each other a few times that year.

Looking back, I can see that I was a bit flaky, uncertain of who I was and what I wanted in a relationship. I didn't like feeling that way, but I assumed it was because I grew up without a father in my life. That was one reason why I wanted to get past the trauma of what it meant in my life to lose my father at a young age. Justin always seemed certain that I was the one he would marry. I think that scared me. *How did he know, and why didn't I have that same "knowing feeling"?*

The summer after my first year of college, I went on the mission trip to Macau. Justin moved back in with his parents that summer and worked. I needed time to think about my next steps, so we broke up. I also wanted time to think and focus on this opportunity to serve God overseas. I ended up pondering the relationship all summer. At the end of the summer, I decided the Lord was leading me to pursue the relationship with Justin if he was still interested. He also wanted to continue to pursue me and ended up moving to Boise to be near me.

After I returned from my mission trip to Macau in August and moved back in with my parents, Justin packed up his things and moved to Idaho. We started our engagement in September. It would be a nine-month engagement with a lot of ups and downs. I wish I could say it went amazingly smooth, but it was rough. The rough engagement, in my opinion, can be summed up like this: insecurities, immaturity, and hormones. It felt like an emotional roller coaster half the time. Plus, when something good is about to happen, who but the enemy comes in to try to destroy it?

The wedding day finally came. It was beautiful, and everything went as planned except the part where we were to get the rings. I thought it would be neat to have the rings tied to the pillow the ringbearer, who happened to be my half-brother, was carrying. The rings were still there when we went to get them off the pillow, but someone (my stepdad) had tied them to the pillow in knots. As hard as we tried, we could not get them untied from the delicate, lacy, heart-shaped pillow. Finally, the pastor announced that if anyone in the audience had a pocketknife, could they please bring it up. Fortunately, my soon-to-be husband's old boss had one. Maybe this was staged, but he walked up to the front of the church, not with a small pocketknife but with a large meat-cutting knife. There were laughs all around as we successfully retrieved the wedding rings from the ringbearer's pillow.

When we look back at the wedding video, we can see that as I stooped to get the rings, I looked up and sent a glare toward my stepdad, who seemed to be so proud of himself. He accomplished what he had desired. He had the biggest grin on his face, and he was chuckling so gaily.

We were glad the ordeal was over and continued the ceremony with no other delays. Finally, the seemingly long ceremony ended. We did it: we were now Mr. and Mrs. Justin Dighans.

After a rocky honeymoon consisting of not having enough money and us having an almost love-hate relationship again due to insecurities, immaturity, and hormones, I was finding out it's hard to love another person when you don't really love yourself. I was a perfectionist, and so when things didn't go how I thought they should, I was upset. I also wasn't completely comfortable with my body, so I wanted to be with my new husband sexually and intimately, but I didn't want to be fully seen. This was just what I was feeling; my husband had his own stuff going on that I would discover about a month into our marriage.

We finished the honeymoon with love in our eyes and a smile on our faces, ready to get back to work and be in our home together. Our first home was a triplex unit in Idaho.

About a month after we got home, we were settled into our jobs and getting used to married life. I got a call while I was at work. No, there were no cell phones then; this was on the work number to the office I worked in. It was our life insurance agent. He was calling to let me know that the results from my husband's insurance physical had come back, and there was tobacco in his blood.

My heart sank as I thought I had married a saint, not a sinner. *Why didn't I know about him using tobacco?* Well, one thing I knew was that he wasn't a smoker; I was certain he wouldn't have been able to keep that from me. How did he keep it a secret that he chewed tobacco? All the questions came. Why didn't he tell me? Doesn't he love me? Can I trust him anymore? What else isn't he telling me? I thought we had shared everything. How could we move forward from there?

This situation took us on a path of me trying to get him to stop chewing tobacco. I would say, "You need to stop; it's wrong," or "It's not good for your health," or "Stop for me," or "Just stop!" Then, of course, he felt attacked. I also questioned his faith. "Spend more time with God," I would push. "Did you have your devotions this morning?" I would inquire. He would get angry. He would stop chewing for a little while and then start up again without telling me. I didn't understand addiction, and I would tell him, "Just let me know if you start again" or "If you're feeling the urge to start again, just tell me so we can work together." He wouldn't let me know, so then it would start all the distress over again. I would think he had stopped, then learn he had started again. And again, I would question if I could trust him and if he loved me. We would go in circles like this on and off for over ten years.

I know, I know, I am a slow learner, but I did finally learn after we had our sixth baby. I realized that I couldn't continue struggling with this. It was between him and God. I took a step one afternoon and called a well-known "call-in counseling" service. I spoke to a counselor about what was going on. I don't remember exactly how he counseled me or how he said it, but I do remember getting off the phone and realizing I had to make a choice. I could either keep hounding my husband about this situation and continue to struggle in the marriage, or I could love him right where he was at and stop pushing and trying to control him. I needed to stop trying to make him into something he wasn't. I talked to one other pastor about the situation, and he just said, "Everyone has something they struggle with." Again, I realized I had to leave it and just do me and keep loving him.

That is exactly what I did, and the results were amazing. You know what was interesting? After I gave up that fight and let go of any bitterness with his tobacco use and our conflicts about it, I was healed physically in one area that I had specifically been asking God about.

After my third baby, Luke, I had developed varicose veins. With my fourth, fifth, and sixth babies, I was uncomfortable during those pregnancies because of the vein situation. If I stood for long, my legs, especially one of them, would throb. I would have to stand on one foot for a few minutes to relieve the pain. This would be my routine while cooking dinner. I would get it started, then lift my throbbing foot for a few minutes until the pain eased. Then I would stand on it for a few minutes again and repeat lifting the throbbing foot for a bit. This would go on until I decided to ask for more help from the kids, or my husband would get home and insist that I go put my feet up. I would then lie on the couch with my legs elevated until dinner was ready. If I was walking and moving, it would feel a bit better, but standing for long periods was painful. I would wear compression socks during my pregnancies and during my monthly cycle between pregnancies for those years. The compression socks helped but did not cure it, by any means.

When I got pregnant with my seventh baby, Jaclyn, I realized I had little to no pain in my legs. I believe healing came because of my spiritual growth and because I had chosen to let go of the strife and bitterness toward my husband. Look at this verse:

"Beloved, I pray that in every way you may succeed and prosper and be in good health [physically], just as [I know] your soul prospers [spiritually]." 3 John 1:2

I recalled asking the Lord to heal my veins and take away the pain. The previous summer, I was led to prepare a mostly raw food diet for our family and me. I believe I was also led to do that to help bring about this healing. The Word says:

"You ask [God for something] and do not receive it, because you ask with wrong motives [out of selfishness or with an unrighteous agenda], so that [when you get what you want] you may spend it on your [hedonistic] desires." James 4:3

I asked Him to take care of the varicose veins and for the pain to go away so that I could better serve Him and others. Then I believed. I didn't know when the healing would manifest in my body, but I didn't have to know when. I just rested and was patient, knowing He hears my cry and He answers me.

> *"In all your ways know and acknowledge and recognize Him, and He will make your paths straight and smooth [removing obstacles that block your way]." Proverbs 3:6*

I recognized that the varicose vein pain was an obstacle blocking my way. I acknowledged Him, and He made my paths straight. In what ways do you need Him to make your paths straight and smooth? Are you willing to ask, listen, obey, and believe?

YOUR NEXT STEPS JOURNALING

_____

_____

_____

_____

_____

_____

_____

_____

_____

_____

_____

_____

_____

_____

_____

_____

_____

_____

_____

_____

_____

_____

_____

_____

_____

_____

CHAPTER 4

I GET TO LIVE!

I had three kids, and she had three kids. Why do I get to live?

My sister, just three years older than me, had a pain in her chest after coming home from an airplane trip with her one-year-old daughter. She thought she had just pulled a muscle or something, but the pain wasn't going away. She decided to get it checked. The results came back as breast cancer. Yes, that word "cancer." *How could this be? She is only thirty years old. She is still nursing her baby. This doesn't make sense.* Those were the words and thoughts running through my mind as she began her journey.

Right away, surgery was scheduled to remove the lump. Next, the treatment would start. She endured many rounds of chemotherapy and then many rounds of radiation. Everything happened so quickly, as though she were being pushed through from one procedure to the next. From my perspective, it seemed like there was no time to look at other options or even process what was going on. I sensed her state of fear and the thought, "This has to be taken care of now." Maybe I felt that way because I was living in another state when all this was going on. Whatever it was, a sense of urgency was in the air, and there was no wasting time or pausing to evaluate the next best step. Reports were coming in and decisions were being made quickly, at least that was what I saw from my position.

Since I walked through this medical issue with my sister, I have become more aware that we do have choices about our health and our medical treatments. It's not always wise to just go with what one doctor says. We do have a say in what is being done to our body, and we can even say, "No, I'm not doing that." Doctors are amazing, and I am thankful for their services, but we must be people who pay attention to the Holy Spirit on the inside of us and do what God is leading us to do. We must not just be people who are pushed forward by our own or others' emotions or bad reports from the doctor.

I believe in prayer and the healing power of God. I also believe in the laying on of hands and speaking the name of Jesus over our lives. Natural medicine is another amazing option, as well as the conventional medicine route. What is most important in all this is that we do it the way God is telling us to. The picture is so much bigger than we may think. The places we go, the people we meet, and the supplement or medicine we take are all for a much greater purpose. This awareness makes our lives as believers so rich, full, and adventurous. We carry the God of the universe on the inside of us. We must realize the power we carry and walk in it wherever we go, whatever we are doing.

> *"Trust in and rely confidently on the Lord with all your heart. And do not rely on your own insight or understanding. In all your ways know and acknowledge and recognize Him, And He will make your paths straight and smooth [removing obstacles that block your way]." Proverbs 3:5–6*

Not long after all this came up with my sister's health, the Lord prompted my husband and me to move our family from Montana back to Idaho. We had moved to Montana about five years before when my husband had gotten a job with an electrical company there. We were enjoying our life in Montana but did not feel tied to anything there at that point. I have lived most of my life being available to God, willing to go wherever He calls.

We found out that my husband, being an electrician by trade, could easily get a job with the company he had left several years before in Idaho. We put our home on the market, packed up, and moved. We rented a house in Idaho that was near the rest of the family who lived there. I had another sister and her family there, as well as my mom, stepdad, and half-brother.

We were led to move back to help, encourage, and be with the family at this time. Our move happened in the summer, and our kids weren't school age yet. Everything flowed smoothly as we moved our family of five, at that point, to another state.

At Christmas, we couldn't attend the family gathering due to our family having slight colds. My sister had a compromised immune system, and we respected her situation and chose to stay home.

I made it special at our house. We went out caroling to our extended family members' homes. We wanted to be a blessing and encouragement, so we did what we could during that time. I also wanted to be intentional with my kids and show them it wasn't a bad thing that we couldn't join the Christmas gathering. I chose to look for other opportunities rather than go toward discouragement. If you really look at it, discouragement is the easy route. That is what people generally choose when plans change or don't go the way they were thinking. What would it look like if we learned to be flexible people? How would that change the outcome when things don't go as planned? What if you could pivot and look for new opportunities in the situation at hand?

While we were living in Idaho during my sister's illness, I was there to help my sister cut her hair when it started falling out. The first week, we cut it shoulder length. She had beautiful, long, wavy hair, and as it started falling out, it was easier to deal with at a shorter length. Next, I helped her cut it short, close to her head. She wore scarves for a couple of weeks as the hair-falling-out process came to an end. Then she ordered a wig. The first one was like her natural hair had been: long and wavy. At first, she wanted it as much like her natural hair as possible. She liked it that way for a short season. It quickly became more of a bother, getting in the way and itchy. The next one she ordered a few months later was a cute, short style that was much more comfortable. This process was not easy to walk through with her, but I am thankful I had that time with my sister.

I also remember helping her with organizing, cleaning, and getting rid of things. I wanted her to know I was there for her and that I loved her. I did my best to get that across. The extended family time we had during my sister's illness was priceless. I am so thankful we made that a priority for what ended up being about six months. At that point, we had been paying for rent and our house payment ever since we moved. Our house in Montana still hadn't sold. We decided that since my sister was in a better spot and had been through the hardest part of the treatment, we were free to go back to Montana. So, we did.

A few months later, another tumor was found. This time, it was on my sister's brain behind her ear. It was brain cancer. Surgery was scheduled. She didn't come out of that surgery as well. She had a hard time swallowing, and her voice was softer than normal and sounded different because of where the tumor was located. She was unstable when she walked, at times needing a cane.

I traveled back and forth for occasional visits. I would call her almost daily and read verses to her to encourage her. After a long, two-year battle with cancer, she passed away.

As I watched her walk through this, I was asking God questions and making commitments in my heart. I cried out to God, "Why do I get to live? She has three kids; I have three kids." I realized what a privilege it is to have life and get to raise my kids and be a wife. I realized how precious life is, and I wanted to do my best job at it. Again, I called out, "Lord, help me live my life well." I started asking God more about what my life should look like. I wanted more joy with my children. I wanted to make everything I did count. All of it. Asking God questions can be intimidating, but it can also open a whole new life for the person willing to do it. I began realizing that it wasn't my life I was living but Him living through me as I learned to yield to Him.

What would happen if you got curious about why you're feeling a certain way or why you have what you have in your life? What if you looked at your thoughts and changed them? I can tell you from experience that it will completely change your life if you let it.

It was a privilege to speak at my sister's funeral. Words just came, and I reminisced about her and all she brought to our family, her family, and her world. She was a blessing to those who knew her.

The following verses came up as I was talking with the Lord about what I would say.

> *"Yet you do not know [the least thing] about what may happen in your life tomorrow. [What is secure in your life?] You are merely a vapor [like a puff of smoke or a wisp of steam from a cooking pot] that is visible for a little while and then vanishes [into thin air]." James 4:14*

> *"He said, Listen carefully, all [you people of] Judah, and you inhabitants of Jerusalem, and King Jehoshaphat. The Lord says this to you: 'Be not afraid or dismayed at this great multitude, for the battle is not yours, but God's.'" 2 Chronicles 20:15*

Four years later, my sister's husband, my brother-in-law, also passed away from brain cancer. This was another shock to the family. Their three kids would then live with my mom and stepdad, their grandparents. At this point, they were all elementary age. My parents had taken care of the kids a lot prior to the death of their father. Thankfully, these children were familiar with their grandparents and this home they would now call their own. They all continued at the same schools and church and with the same friends. Later, they all graduated from high school. Unfortunately, the middle child got into drugs and ended up passing away of a drug overdose a couple of years after graduation. My sister's other two kids earned college degrees and are doing well.

I learned so much through these trials. I saw my sister, just three years older than me, battle cancer and move from this life to the next life. I watched her family being left without a mother and then without a father. Yet, God provided a wonderful place for them. I witnessed her child struggling with addiction leading to death. I realized that I had a choice of how I emerged from yet another trial. This was the fourth death of a close family member. I was able to continue a normal life on the outside, but on the inside, God was doing a work. I was allowing Him to mold and shape me into the person He wanted me to be. My life was not my own. I was on a journey of yielding myself to Him. At first, I would call it surrendering to Him, but surrendering is what a person does with an enemy. Yielding is laying my life down to allow Him to lead. It's slowing down and putting aside my agenda so that His life is lived out through me.

"Dear brothers and sisters, when troubles of any kind come your way, consider it an opportunity for great joy. For you know that when your faith is tested, your endurance has a chance to grow. So let it grow, for when your endurance is fully developed, you will be perfect and complete, needing nothing." James 1:2–4 (NLT)

Know that the testing of your faith will produce something. What will you allow the trials that you face to produce in you? If you choose the high road, the yielded road, they will make you mature and complete, lacking nothing. We all have a choice. What will you choose to do when you face trials of many kinds? We will never be without them, but we get to decide how we go through them. What if you allowed yourself to grow?

"I am the Vine; you are the branches. The one who remains in Me and I in him bears much fruit, for [otherwise] apart from Me [that is, cut off from vital union with Me] you can do nothing." John 15:5

The yielded life is the best life. What would it take for you to step toward living a yielded life in Christ? What thoughts would you have to think? Is your life going the way you want it to go? Or are you being shaken by every trial that comes your way? You will be moved and shaken by every trial unless you yield yourself to God today and allow Him to mold and shape you with each trouble that comes.

> *"For in Him we live and move and exist [that is, in Him we actually have our being], as even some of your own poets have said, 'For we also are His children.'" Acts 17:28*

> *"I have told you these things, so that in Me you may have [perfect] peace. In the world you have tribulation and distress and suffering, but be courageous [be confident, be undaunted, be filled with joy]; I have overcome the world." [My conquest is accomplished, My victory abiding.]" John 16:33*

After letting go of all the control you think you have, yielding to God brings so much freedom and joy!

MOVING FORWARD JOURNALING

_____

_____

_____

_____

_____

_____

_____

_____

_____

_____

_____

_____

_____

_____

_____

_____

_____

_____

_____

_____

_____

_____

CHAPTER 5

OVERWHELMED WITH THREE KIDS

Shortly after my sister's death, I met a mom with six kids. She homeschooled them, and she seemed happy and like she was enjoying her children. I questioned, "You seem so happy with six kids. I have three children, and I'm overwhelmed. How do you do it?" She smiled and said, "Children are such a blessing." I pondered that. I knew the Bible talked about children being a gift and a reward from Him.

> "Behold, children are a heritage and gift from the Lord, the fruit of the womb a reward." Psalm 127:3

Why wasn't I experiencing them as a gift and a reward? I was overwhelmed, anxious, and frustrated a lot of the time. It felt like I couldn't enjoy them as much as I tried. I knew it wasn't because of them and what they were doing. After all, they were just being children and needed discipline and training. I knew it was because of my mindset and thoughts. I came to realize how hard it is for a person to love anyone else when they don't love themself. That was exactly where I was with my children. I felt unable to love them well. It felt like something was blocking my ability to love them fully. I realized I didn't love myself, so how could I love others?

> *"'Teacher, which is the greatest commandment in the Law?' And Jesus replied to him, 'You shall love the Lord your God with all your heart, and with all your soul, and with all your mind.' This is the first and greatest commandment. The second is like it, 'You shall love your neighbor as yourself [that is, unselfishly seek the best or higher good for others].'" Matthew 22:36–39*

> *"If, however, you are [really] fulfilling the royal law according to the Scripture, 'you shall love your neighbor as yourself [that is, if you have an unselfish concern for others and do things for their benefit]' you are doing well." James 2:8*

God brought me on a journey to fall in love with Him so I could love myself and my husband, children, and others. I call it "live loving and being loved." The way I fell in love with God is by taking the time to get to know Him. I came to a point in my life where I desperately needed Him. To this day, I cannot live without Him. He is my Vital Need. I have seen Him do so much in my life, and I am so thankful for all He has done.

I also had to allow myself to receive God's love for me and believe He loves me before I could say "I love myself." I had to get to that spot of living "being loved." From there, it became easier to love my husband, children, and others. The hardest spot to get to is to receive God's love for ourselves. The reason a person isn't willing to receive God's love is because they don't see their worth. We know all the "stuff" in our lives, and we don't think we are worthy or deserving of His love. The amazing truth is that we don't have to feel worthy; we just have to be open to receiving God's love, even when we feel yucky. We need to be able to say thank you to Him for His love. It is a gift. A "just because" gift. A "while we were still sinners" gift. Will you receive it and be open to His amazing, unconditional love? If you won't, you are saying no to Him because He is Love. You can't do anything to earn it; you can only receive it freely.

*"But God clearly shows and proves His own love for us,
by the fact that while we were still sinners, Christ died for
us." Romans 5:8*

Wow! Isn't that amazing love? Don't you just want to
bask in it? You are loved. When you start from a place of
being loved, it allows us to respond to people and
circumstances in life so much better.

Back to this mom with her six kids. I asked her about
homeschooling. I had not yet started that venture
because all our kids were still preschool age. I asked her
why she had a big family. Again, the response was
basically "Children are such a blessing."

She gave me a book about a mom who homeschooled
her ten children. In the book, the author shared how they
came to the decision to have a large family. She shared
what their family homeschool life was like. Her story
greatly inspired me.

After reading that book, I felt a pull toward having a large
family. I had no idea why, but I knew that God gives us
the desires of our hearts. Because I had that desire, I acted
on it. That first step was to ask the Lord if this was for
me and us. Here again, I asked the Lord about what I was
thinking. I got curious as to why I was feeling a pull

toward having a large family. I was from a family of four children, and my husband was from a family of three children.

My next step, of course, was to ask my husband what he thought about the idea of having a large family. To tell you the truth, the thought excited me and scared me at the same time. He said, "Sure." At that point in his life, having more sex was right up his alley. Why wouldn't he say, "Sure"? I don't think either of us had a clue what we were saying yes to.

Right then and there, we decided to go toward having a large family. "One at a time" is the way we said we would go about it. We didn't have a number in mind; it was just one at a time. And that is exactly how it turned out. One baby at a time until we reached ten children in nineteen years. I basically had a baby every other year for nineteen years. I was either nursing or pregnant for almost two decades. I remember asking my husband after each baby, "Do you want to have another one?" At first, I would wait a few months to a year before I could ask him if he wanted another one, mostly because I needed to make sure I wanted to go through that process again. I needed to get past the emotion of having the latest one and all the changes a new baby added to the family. I remember being shocked after my seventh baby that I desired to have another baby right away so much that I voiced it while I was still in the hospital.

I look back on those years now, and WOW! At the time of this writing, I have three kids who are married, two granddaughters, one grandson, one grandbaby on the way, and seven kids still at home. Yes, we have had years that were a blur, but I'm in awe and amazed at God's goodness. What a full life. I wouldn't change it for anything. Without this path, without raising this large family, without all the trials, I would have never reached the place of leaning and relying on God as I do. It's an awesome and amazing place to be. We all have a path in life, and it's for a reason. Our past is preparing us for our future. Allow what you go through to draw you near to God. Like the Scripture says:

> *"Draw near to God and He will draw near to you. Cleanse your hands, you sinners; and purify your hearts, you double-minded." James 4:8 (NKJV)*

This is what happened to me. As I sought the Lord, drawing near to Him, He met me right there. He, in turn, drew near to me. It's a beautiful relationship. Make sure you grow through the trials you go through. Choosing to grow through your trials will make you mature and complete, lacking nothing.

One thought I often have as I walk through trials is "I don't want to have to go through this again the same way." It's not that I believe I won't have trials, but when I go through a trial again, I want to go through it stronger and with less pain and more peace. I want to go through it with God, leaning on Him, relying on Him, trusting Him, and not being shaken or moved by the trial. That's why my motto is: I don't want to go through the same thing the same way again.

I encourage you to recognize the growth that can happen through your trials. Make the trial count. Be intentional about it drawing you near to God. Be intentional about growing through what you are going through. Recognize what God is showing you about Himself through the storms of life. What if you consider it pure joy as you face trials, knowing that the testing of your faith will make you mature and complete, lacking nothing?

"My brethren, count it all joy when you fall into various trials, knowing that the testing of your faith produces patience. But let patience have its perfect work, that you may be perfect and complete, lacking nothing." James 1:2-4 (NKJV)

YOUR NEXT STEPS JOURNALING

_____

_____

_____

_____

_____

_____

_____

_____

_____

_____

_____

_____

_____

_____

_____

_____

_____

_____

_____

_____

_____

_____

_____

CHAPTER 6

DEPRESSED TO BLESSED

O ur oldest daughter, Jayna, went to public kindergarten in Bozeman, Montana. It was a great year for her, and I enjoyed going into the classroom once a week to help. I would always take our four-year-old, our second daughter, Summer, with me. After that school year, we moved back to the town where I had grown up. It was the town where my husband and I had met, the town with a lot of memories, both good and bad.

My husband's parents were ready to sell the greenhouse business they had started several years before. We decided this would be a positive move for us as a family. We took them up on the offer.

I was a bit uneasy about this move. I had lived in this small town for almost fifteen years while growing up. A lot of hard stuff had happened in those years that made me wonder what it would feel like to live there again. I didn't let those fears get in the way of what newness God may have for us back in that old spot. I thought I should be a different person since I was almost fifteen years older. Couldn't the old spot be made new? I decided I would give it a try. I didn't want fear to be a deciding factor in my life. I wanted to get past my fears.

Around the time we decided to make the move, we also decided to homeschool our children. Again, we would take it one year at a time. We had four children when we moved. I wanted to learn to relate to my children well, and I felt a homeschool lifestyle would assist with that desire. We also thought that with the business we would be taking over, our summers would be busier. We desired a family business, so homeschooling seemed like a great option for this reason too.

A homeschool family we became. We joined a homeschool group, bought a curriculum, and set up the house. I made the schedule, we had a plan, and the journey started. I followed a routine religiously but also flexibly since we added a baby to the household every other year. We did book work in the mornings, and the afternoons would consist of quiet time in the house with the baby and younger kids napping and the older ones having quiet playtime in their rooms. When they were old enough, they could go to work with Dad, do projects in the garage, work on outside chores, or play.

I would spend the afternoons resting, folding clothes, or doing other quiet chores while watching or listening to DVDs or CDs on marriage, parenting, large family logistics, or spiritual growth. I enjoyed reading faith-based books on these subjects as well.

I started homeschooling our four children. One school age, one preschooler, a toddler, and a baby. I read books on how to structure a homeschool day with many different ages. I was considered a naturally organized person, but I learned and grew a lot in this area over the years. I was constantly writing schedules and plans to make each year go more smoothly. I remember being intentional about my job as a teacher and homeschool mom. I learned to dress for my day, putting myself together before the children got up. I learned how important it was for me to be ready mentally and physically for my children.

When I had five kids, I went through a time of depression. I had gone through depression before, but this time stood out. I had just had my fifth baby, Alena. She was another beautiful, healthy baby.

When she was just about a week old, I remember walking down to our greenhouse, which was right on our property, with the five kids. I was holding Alena in my arms. It was about 6:30 p.m., closing time for the greenhouse. I was looking forward to having my husband home for the evening. Engaging with an adult and having someone else help with the kids was sounding very good after a busy day of homeschooling with four kids and tending to a new baby.

As we approached my husband, he was looking focused, not really like he was closing up for the day. I saw him loading a truck and trailer, which usually meant he was preparing for the next landscape job. I said, "Hey Hun, the greenhouse is closed. Are you about ready to come back for dinner?" He looked at me with those focused "on-a-mission eyes" and said, "No, I'm going to finish a landscape job." My heart sank; he didn't understand. I needed him to come home. I needed help with the kids. I needed him to take the baby or the kids and create a change in the atmosphere. He, on the other hand, was focused on providing for the family. His mind was on doing the next job and getting the next paycheck.

I shuffled back to the house with our five kids, Alena still in my arms. I was disappointed and upset. I would need to continue caring for the children myself. As I walked back, I was creating a new plan for my evening. I knew I still needed to show up for the children. They still needed to be tended to. My husband, on the other hand, went to finish the job. He was torn between coming home and finishing the job. He was torn between spending time with the children and me and getting the next paycheck. I knew something needed to change. I couldn't continue the way I was handling things, and he couldn't continue the way he was doing things.

During this time, anxiety, depression, and fear were growing in my life. Meanwhile, stress, anger, and overwhelm were growing in his life. I was relating to him in unhealthy ways and putting unrealistic expectations on him. What I needed to do was learn to go to my Heavenly Father with many of those expectations and needs instead of going to my husband. Over the years, I would learn this, but right now, it was all I knew. It was making my life hard, and it was putting pressure on our relationship.

This season of having my fifth and sixth babies was the hardest. It wasn't because they were difficult babies. It was hard because I was in a difficult spot personally. I was allowing fear to rule my life rather than the truth of the Word of God. My husband was also in a difficult spot. He was chasing the paycheck, dealing with employees, and stacking everything on his shoulders rather than trusting God. I always said I never had difficult babies. If things seemed difficult, it was because of my mental, emotional and spiritual state.

If I was stressed, the baby would sense it. If I was uptight, the kids would know it and act up. I knew I needed to get to a place of peace. But how? I knew I could go to the doctor to get on an antidepressant. We are free to decide, right? But that wasn't the direction I felt the Lord leading me. I knew that getting on an antidepressant would not heal me or fix the problem; it would merely cover it. I didn't want to just be bandaged. I wanted to be characterized by peace and joy, and I wanted my life completely changed.

I wanted lasting, true results. How would I get the results I wanted? I continued to seek God and ask Him about what I desired. After all, I called myself a believer. I had accepted the Lord at a young age. I had my Bible and my devotionals—lots of them. If I really believed that the Word of God was true, then I could expect to get results in my life if I applied it to my life, right? One verse I knew was:

> *"For the word of God is living and active and full of power [making it operative, energizing, and effective]. It is sharper than any two-edged sword, penetrating as far as the division of the soul and spirit [the completeness of a person], and of both joints and marrow [the deepest parts of our nature], exposing and judging the very thoughts and intentions of the heart." Hebrews 4:12*

If the Word is alive, then I need to treat it that way. I dove into the Word headfirst. I decided I would start doing everything the Word of God said. My thought was that if I call myself a believer, then I need to act like one.

The first thing I specifically did was check my heart to see if I needed to forgive anyone or ask forgiveness from anyone. I searched my heart, and I went to a couple of people and made things right. I cleared my heart. It was my first step toward purifying my heart before God and man.

> *"Whenever you stand praying, if you have anything against anyone, forgive him [drop the issue, let it go], so that your Father who is in heaven will also forgive you your transgressions and wrongdoings [against Him and others]." Mark 11:25*

I was struggling with depression, feeling down, and not having any joy. I was doing all I could to come out of this depressed state. I was trying to enjoy being with my kids and playing with them, but something was blocking my joy. I couldn't enjoy myself, and it wasn't because of the kids. Something in me was keeping me from feeling joy and peace. In my struggle, I came across this verse:

> *"This [day in which God has saved me] is the day which the Lord has made; Let us rejoice and be glad in it." Psalm 118:24*

If the Lord told us in the Word to rejoice in the day, I would do that. It didn't say if it's a good day, rejoice, or if everything goes as planned, then rejoice, or if there's no trouble, go ahead and rejoice. It simply says: rejoice and be glad because He made the day. I realized that I needed to choose to rejoice in each day, no matter what the day brought. I could rejoice in it because He had made the day. He made each day, and that, in itself, is reason to rejoice.

I had been struggling with even getting out of bed. Thoughts like: "What will I do with the kids?" or "I don't know what to do with the kids," or "What if I make a mistake with them?" would come to mind. I was, in a sense, afraid of the kids. "How will I discipline them?" I was afraid I would do it wrong. So, I didn't want to get up. Fear had paralyzed me.

That verse, Psalm 118:24, got me out of bed. I started saying it first thing when I woke up in the morning as I felt the fear come over me. I didn't only say it, though, I said it with belief, with faith. This is key in the life of a believer.

> *"But without faith it is impossible to [walk with God and] please Him, for whoever comes near to God must [necessarily] believe that God exists and that He rewards those who [earnestly and diligently] seek Him." Hebrews 11:6*

Then I would say it again as I picked myself up off the bed. Then again as each of my children got up. I would paste a smile on my face and say the verse to each of them as I hugged and greeted them each morning. After a week or two, I didn't need to paste on my smile anymore. The depression was gone, and I greeted my children with a genuine smile. I still have that verse in my heart today. I don't need to say it daily because rejoicing in each day has become a habit, and smiling all day has become a habit. There's no more fear in the day for me. Now rejoicing in the day is the only option in my life. Praise God. I am forever grateful for this truth in my life. This truth has made such a difference in the way I live.

This is the day the Lord has made. I will rejoice and be glad in it. Do you need to renew your mind with this verse? Have you been struggling with depression, fear, anxiety, or overwhelm? These issues are real. It's just as real, though, to choose to follow the Word and see the day through His eyes. Each day has so many opportunities for us to grow. How will believing and doing this verse change your life?

Sometime after this enlightenment, my husband and I went to a parenting conference, where we were encouraged to start blessing our children. I immediately grabbed ahold of that concept. For years, I have spoken this blessing over my children:

"The Lord bless you, and keep you [protect you, sustain you, and guard you]; The Lord make his face shine upon you [with favor], And be gracious to you [surrounding you with lovingkindness]; The Lord lift up His countenance (face) upon you [with divine approval], And give you peace [a tranquil heart and life]." Numbers 6:24–26

Here's what it looks like when I speak this blessing over them: I picture His face shining on my children. I picture Him turning his face toward them and giving them peace. I usually touch each of them or embrace them while I speak this over them.

A couple of birthdays ago, my fourteen-year-old daughter got me a gift. It was a beautiful wall hanging of this verse. Obviously, these were precious words in her life. We hung it above our fireplace in our dining room.

I still say this blessing almost every night to one or more of my children. A couple of them will often ask me to say it over them before they go to bed if I haven't already initiated blessing them. Then I encourage them to say it with me. I don't want them to rely on me and my faith; I want them to see that when I am not around to say it to them, they can speak it over themselves and believe that the living words will affect their lives. It is so important for me to not only model Christian living but also to encourage them to make it their own. I believe the Word so much that I need it to go before my family and me. How about you?

Does this idea of blessing your children stir up anything in you? If so, do it, even if it feels uncomfortable or your children look at you like you are crazy. Why would we let "uncomfortable" make our decision for us?

A couple of years ago, this blessing came out as a song, "The Blessing." It was the season my husband was gone more than he was home. I wasn't sure what was happening with our marriage and family at that time. This song, the words of the blessing from Numbers 6, brought new life and hope to me as our family went through some of the most difficult times in our lives. We would play it while we were around the dining room table, and we would sing and worship the Lord. I would raise my hands and imagine all of it happening to our family. It's powerful. I encourage you to do what's on your heart. Don't worry about what anyone thinks. Our words are so important, and they make a huge difference in the outcomes of our lives and the lives of our family members.

It's amazing what the Word of God does when we apply it to our lives. What scriptures do you need to apply to your life and family? Do not delay the blessing it will bring to your life.

MOVING FORWARD JOURNALING

_____

_____

_____

_____

_____

_____

_____

_____

_____

_____

_____

_____

_____

_____

_____

_____

_____

_____

_____

_____

_____

_____

_____

_____

_____

CHAPTER 7

FULL DAYS,

LESSONS LEARNED

During my years of homeschooling and raising our large family, the Lord taught me so much. I remember having several conversations with fellow homeschool moms. I will tell you about some of them in this chapter and tell you the verses God gave me so I could renew my mind in these areas.

One of the conversations was about which curriculum we should use to educate our children. Each year, the same questions came up. This question would be in the back of my mind all year. I could feel the heaviness of this thought weighing on me and on some of the other moms in my circle.

The conversations would go like this: What curriculum are you using? How's it working? What does it cost? Do you like it?

Then the responses would go like this: I don't know if it's right for my child. There must be something better I could try. Maybe I'll try what you are using. This curriculum is so expensive. I can't afford that.

Without ever completely settling the matter, the conversation would continue to center on the concerns and heaviness.

Finally, one day, I was sick and tired of continually going over these questions in my mind. During my devotional time, a verse jumped out at me. I knew it was one that God had brought to me for this situation. It read:

> *"For all who are allowing themselves to be led by the Spirit of God are sons of God." Romans 8:14*

I thought, *Why am I trying to figure out this curriculum question, and why was I not believing that I was led to the right curriculum?*

I knew I was a daughter of God. This verse said that as a daughter of God, I am led by the Spirit of God. I needed to start believing this verse over my life. And it started with believing that the curriculum I was using at the time was right, unless God showed me a different one. This was one more stressor removed from my life. As I applied this verse to this area of my life, the peace quickly spread to many other areas of my life. No more worrying about decisions; I was led by God. I didn't have to keep wondering; now I knew. No more confusion or overthinking; God would show me. I needed to start living like a believer. After all, the Word says I am led by God in every area of my life.

Another frequent conversation was about hoping our kids were getting all they needed educationally, mentally, physically, socially, and spiritually. Of course, I wanted the best for my children. That is one reason I made the decision to homeschool. I felt it was the best place for my kids at the time. I didn't want to be bothered by the thought, *I hope they're getting what they need for their life.* I remember switching this to a thanksgiving prayer. When the thought would come into my mind, I would change it to: *Thank you, Lord, that my children are getting all they need for the life you have for them.*

The Lord also gave me this verse:

> *"All your children shall be taught by the Lord, and great shall be the peace of your children." Isaiah 54:13 (NKJV)*

I started to believe this. I really needed the encouragement of this verse because as hard as I tried to do what I knew to do with my children's education and their child-rearing, life still happened in the Dighans' home. We had a baby every other year, and there was always a toddler in the house and a preschooler around. Kids don't always cooperate perfectly. A lot of other training was going on, along with the chores and the traditional book-work education. All of it is equally important to grow well-rounded children. I had to learn to be flexible and flow in my homeschool days; otherwise, I would have been all bound up, anxious, and overwhelmed all the time. This truth settled my worries and allowed me so much freedom in my homeschool hours and my life. I was learning to trust God, to rest in Him. All too often, we continue to worry and have anxiety over our daily lives, and I was done with that.

Another struggle I was personally having concerned my vision for my family versus what I was seeing happen in our home. The sibling rivalry was at an all-time high, and it bothered me. My marriage wasn't where I wanted it to be. My home needed to run more efficiently. I had about six kids at the time, and I was led by the Lord to believe this verse for my family:

> *"Now to Him who is able to [carry out His purpose and] do superabundantly more than all that we dare ask or think [infinitely beyond our greatest prayers, hopes, or dreams], according to His power that is at work within us, to Him be the glory in the church and in Christ Jesus throughout all generations forever and ever. Amen."*
> *Ephesians 3:20–21*

I believed He would do Ephesians 3:20 in me and my family, my marriage, and my home. I believed He would do exceedingly abundantly far above all I could dare ask or think. More than I could imagine. It starts with believing the Word and resting in the Word. Knowing that He's got this. Are you a believer? Then act like one and believe.

I started rolling my cares over on Him according to this verse:

"Casting all your cares [all your anxieties, all your worries, and all your concerns, once and for all] on Him, for He cares about you [with deepest affection, and watches over you very carefully]." 1 Peter 5:7

I realized that I could keep being weighed down by all the cares, or I could give them to God. Pride and fear keep us from giving our cares to God. We think we can do a better job, and we don't trust Him. We become double-minded and unstable in all we do when we doubt.

"But he must ask [for wisdom] in faith, without doubting [God's willingness to help], for the one who doubts is like a billowing surge of the sea that is blown about and tossed by the wind. For such a person ought not to think or expect that he will receive anything [at all] from the Lord, being a double minded man, unstable and restless in all his ways [in everything he thinks, feels, or decides]." James 1:6–8

Believing is so important. That's what faith is about, and it's our work as Christians, according to John 6:28-29. If we are not believing, why do we even bother with God and the Bible at all? It's more frustrating to live lukewarm. God hates it when we are lukewarm and said to be either hot or cold, or He will spit us out.

"So because you are lukewarm (spiritually useless), and neither hot nor cold, I will vomit you out of my mouth [rejecting you with disgust]." Revelation 3:16

I personally don't want to be spiritually useless. I want God and all of Him in my life and working in my family with full power. Why even do something if you are only going to do it halfway? Live this Christian life to the fullest. Walk it out; share it with others. Live real and raw. Believe God and don't step away from that belief. Is it working any other way? If so, do it that way, but I guarantee it will only work for a short time, and then you will be looking for something else. The only true satisfaction is by going after God 100 percent. I've tried it other ways and have found that nothing else works. How will you get to the point where you are on fire for Him and the assignment He has put you in charge of?

One morning, I was teaching music with my children—our normal routine. The older ones were playing drums, guitar, and keyboard while singing, and the younger ones were running around with their own play instruments. I was holding or nursing the baby while sitting on the couch in the same room. I looked up at the wall where I had a framed verse. It read:

"Unless the Lord builds the house, they labor in vain who build it; Unless the Lord guards the city, the watchman keeps awake in vain." Psalm 127:1

Tears streamed down my face as I asked the Lord to build my house, build my marriage, and build my family. I don't know how I told Him: I don't want to do my life in vain. I didn't want to waste my time in my own thoughts about what to do with my family or marriage or home. It made me sick to think that I could waste my whole life doing my own thing. I wanted to acknowledge God in every area. I've watched Him help me one step at a time as I pay attention to and want His leading.

"In all your ways, know and acknowledge and recognize Him, and He will make your paths straight and smooth [removing obstacles that block your way]." Proverbs 3:6.

It's in the letting go and trusting Him that we find life. Letting go of control, letting go of my way, letting go of perfection, letting go of the what-ifs, and rolling all our cares onto Him that we really begin to live. Not just be alive.

"For whoever wishes to save his life [in this world] will [eventually] lose it [through death], but whoever loses his

life [in this world] for My sake will find it [that is, life with Me for all eternity]." Matthew 16:25

Will you stop doing things in vain? When will you change? If you don't change now, you will be forced to at some point. What do you need to let go of in your life, your marriage, your family, your home, or your business? Letting go and deciding to trust Him will change everything. It will be uncomfortable, but you have to ask yourself if it is working the way you have been doing it. What are you trying to control? Do you realize that the harder you hold on, the quicker it slips out of your hands? Your Heavenly Father really does have your best interest in mind.

On this same topic concerning the success of my children and my life, another truth the Lord showed me was this:

"This Book of the Law shall not depart from your mouth, but you shall read [and meditate on] it day and night, so that you may be careful to do [everything] in accordance with all that is written in it; for then you will make your way prosperous, and then you will be successful." Joshua 1:8

I decided then and there with this verse that for me to make the children's academics a priority over their character and the way I act toward them as a mom would not get them to the goal. It would not get them to God. After all, according to this verse, we see that meditating on the Word makes us prosperous and successful.

I began being more purposeful about teaching my children the Word, memorizing scripture, and saying confessions. I did not always keep the perfect flow. I know there were gaps and areas I missed or could have done better, but I did what I knew at the time. I also see so many great things in my children that I did right. I know I can trust God with this because:

> *"And we know [with great confidence] that God [who is deeply concerned about us] causes all things to work together [as a plan] for good for those who love God, to those who are called according to His plan and purpose."*
> *Romans 8:28*

I have confidence in this. I can continue to do my best in the future. I live my life with no regrets. Why would I question God's goodness? Again, it's about believing the Word. Fellow Christians, we must act like believers.

Your Next Steps Journaling

_____

_____

_____

_____

_____

_____

_____

_____

_____

_____

_____

_____

_____

_____

_____

_____

_____

_____

_____

_____

_____

_____

_____

_____

CHAPTER 8

There Must Be More

A s I continued to grow and be a doer of the Word, I asked the Lord to help me hunger and thirst after righteousness, like the Word tells us to do.

> *"Blessed [joyful, nourished by God's goodness] are those who hunger and thirst for righteousness [those who actively seek right standing with God], for they will be [completely] satisfied." Matthew 5:6*

I asked Him to fill us, my family and me, with the Holy Spirit because the Word tells us to be filled in Ephesians.

"Do not get drunk with wine, for that is wickedness (corruption, stupidity), but be filled with the [Holy] Spirit and constantly guided by Him." Ephesians 5:18

As I asked, He answered. I grew so hungry for more. At first, when I began digging into the Word like this, I felt like I was hanging on to every word I read as if my life depended on it. It felt like I was clinging to the Lord and His Word. If I let go of Him, Who is the Word, I would fall into a deep, dark pit, never to climb out.

I kept clinging and doing everything the Word said to do. I hungered more and more for righteousness. After all, the Word says to draw near to God, and He will draw near to you. Cleanse your hands, you sinners, and purify your hearts, you double-minded. I felt God drawing near to me, and He met me right where I was as I sought Him. He started helping me throw off the weights and sin in my life that were entangling me.

"Therefore, since we are surrounded by so great a cloud of witnesses [who by faith have testified to the truth of God's absolute faithfulness], stripping off every unnecessary weight and the sin which so easily and cleverly entangles us, let us run with endurance and active persistence the race that is set before us." Hebrews 12:1

One weight at a time, I was lightened and freed. I continue to walk in this freedom and keep throwing off weights that may be entangling me as I move forward.

I want to tell you more about what transpired in our lives after I asked the Lord to fill us with the Spirit (Ephesians 5:18). One morning at the breakfast table, I sincerely and full of faith asked the Lord to fill us with the Spirit. The kids and I would pray and memorize scripture around the table as we started our school day. I would teach them what I was learning from the Word. In my prayer that morning, I asked the Lord to fill us with His Spirit. I did not know what to expect except that I knew He would do just what I asked because I love Him and He answers me when I call.

From that time forward, I have watched God bring us out of darkness into His glorious light.

> *"But you are a chosen race, a royal priesthood, a consecrated nation, a [special] people for God's own possession, so that you may proclaim the excellencies [the wonderful deeds and virtues and perfections] of Him who called you out of darkness into His marvelous light."*
> *1 Peter 2:9*

I know we were filled with the Spirit the moment we asked. I didn't have any knowledge of what it meant except that I knew I would see, feel, and have more of God in, with, and among my family and me. I noticed right away that we had more joy. Others noticed too. At about that same time, we went to a family gathering, and one of my relatives commented on how smiley and joyful we all looked. I remember that time, and we were truly filled with joy. I and all of the children radiated it. I was so thankful for what God had done in our lives, filling us with more of Himself because we asked Him to.

We started seeking more and growing in the Word. This caused shifting within us. We were not fitting into our church as we had previously. The Word became clearer and started making more sense to us. We learned about healing and saw it happen in our own lives. We felt more clarity in every area of our lives, and we gained the knowledge of what speaking in tongues meant and understood it to be the evidence of the filling of the Spirit.

I was open to whatever God had for my family and me. I was a homeschool teacher, a mom to several children with plans to have more, and a wife and helper to my husband with our family business. I needed God to show up like He did in the days of Moses. I needed the sea to part for my family and me and for us to walk across on dry ground. No more stumbling around in the mud and muck or having the pressure of enemies on one side and the sea on the other and nowhere to go. If the Word is true and I'm a believer, I will believe the Word and see the results of it. I will see miracles take place in my life. That settled it: there was no room for any other option in my life. Either I believe the Word, or I don't. Either I act like a believer, or I don't. Either the Word is true, or it's not, and if it isn't true, then why waste my time on it?

Well, I'm still a believer, and I still regularly see events happen in my life on a supernatural level. I found what I was looking for: life and life in abundance. It's what Jesus died for. It's what He came to give. The Word says:

> *"Ask and keep on asking and it will be given to you; seek and keep on seeking and you will find; knock and keep on knocking and the door will be opened to you." Matthew 7:7*

> *"For everyone who keeps on asking receives, and he who keeps on seeking finds, and to him who keeps on knocking, it will be opened." Matthew 7:8*

"If you then, evil (sinful by nature) as you are, know how to give good and advantageous gifts to your children, how much more will your Father who is in heaven [perfect as He is] give what is good and advantageous to those who keep on asking Him." Matthew 7:11

"If you, then, being evil [that is, sinful by nature], know how to give good gifts to your children, how much more will your Heavenly Father give the Holy Spirit to those who ask and continue to ask Him!" Luke 11:13

The Lord brought us out of the non-denominational Bible church we had been in for eight years and put us in a spirit-filled church where we were learning about the Holy Spirit, speaking in tongues, healing, and faith. I was open to these areas but didn't know a lot about them.

We had just had our ninth baby, Blaize, when we moved to our new church. It was no small feat getting all the children settled into our new spot. But we did it! We didn't give up. We were all filled with the Spirit with evidence of speaking in tongues. We spiritually grew and learned so much.

I witnessed five differences when we switched to this Spirit-filled church. First, our old friends treated us like we were strangers, and some even wrote opposition letters or debated us. Second, I felt, for the first time, persecution for righteousness's sake. Third, I noticed spiritual warfare in our lives. Fourth, scripture became alive and was easier to understand. Fifth, I noticed more boldness and power in witnessing and sharing the Word. It was such an amazing time of growth and understanding. But also a season full of trials.

It was not easy losing all our friends from our previous church. It felt like they were afraid of us. It's interesting what religion does. It can turn you against your own. Why wouldn't we, as believers, be happy when God is leading our fellow Christians to a different spot? Could that new spot mean growth and direction for them from God? Instead, why do we judge and fear the steps of other believers? Would God be telling you what fellow Christians are supposed to do? Why do we go against other believers when someone leaves their local body for another one? After all, aren't we all part of one Body, the Body of Christ, one Church? I may be stepping on some toes here, but it needs to be said. Our family has experienced this a few times, and it's not a reflection of the heart of God. We need to stop, Church. Let's grow up and be excited for one another and encourage each other in the Lord rather than going into fear and avoiding our brothers and sisters who go to different churches.

Thankfully, we fit right in with this new church and began to grow rapidly. We found kids and families to connect with and activities to get involved with. I am so thankful for all the growth that God showed us and walked us into at this church. We thought we would be with this church forever. But after about eight years, again, we were led to leave this church that we had been so connected to. It was shortly after the pandemic and at the time that I became a Covenant Life Coach. I'll share more about this in another chapter.

MOVING FORWARD JOURNALING

_____

_____

_____

_____

_____

_____

_____

_____

_____

_____

_____

_____

_____

_____

_____

_____

_____

_____

_____

_____

_____

_____

CHAPTER 9

PACK MY BAGS?

W̲e switched over to our new church, and most of us were flourishing. I was so hungry for the Word and growing in it. My husband, on the other hand, was growing but also had a negative attitude. We had just closed a business that had been open for eight years. Our eighth baby, Lindy, was around six months old. My husband was in the beginning stages of a breakdown or depression, or both. He was not medically treated for this except for some high blood pressure medicine, but he only took it for a short time because the side effects were undesirable. I could see my husband so angry and reactive at times, and then at other times, he could sit and watch the leaves on the aspen trees for hours.

His deepest low spot happened between our ninth and tenth children. I wasn't sure what to do, but I prayed and sought the Lord. Since we had just changed churches, I didn't know the pastors or anyone else well enough to try to explain that my husband was struggling badly. Even if I did tell them, what would or could they do? We didn't have family to go to at that time, either. Most of our old friends, as I said earlier, had walked away from us when we switched churches.

As for me, I wasn't sure what was going on with myself, either. God was all I had during this time, and according to the Word, He is enough. He had to be enough. I wasn't seeing or being led to any other options. I had one person who would pray with me, but it wasn't someone I could completely confide in. I didn't want to share all our stuff anyway. I wanted results, not just talk.

I completely surrendered to the Lord. I realized the only way I could make it through and not lose myself was by living in Him. You might be wondering what that means exactly. Let me explain what it meant for me during this devastating time of trials.

The Word tells us we are hidden in Christ. If this is true, then my thought was, *It's Christ that comes to the trouble before me. It hits Him first.* I became hidden in Christ. I specifically remember one night. My husband, Justin, was in a negative mood. He had not emotionally been there as a husband, and he was not interested sexually, either. Negative words toward me were flying out of his mouth as we were going to bed. I realized I couldn't walk through this alone. I had just had my tenth baby, and there wasn't anyone to call on. People have their own difficulties; they don't need to hear mine. I realized that I had God, and I needed to lean on Him as if He were right there. I needed Him to be my husband at this point because my earthly husband was not able to fill that role.

I would pray in the Spirit, worship Him, focus on the Word, listen to sermons online, and say affirmations of who I am and who my husband is. Plus, I would quote other scripture and words that had been spoken in our church or over me directly. I stopped fighting with my husband. I would ask my Father in heaven what to say, and I would say it calmly and clearly.

As I lay in bed that night, I felt God's love surround me so much that the harsh words and sharpness coming from my husband couldn't touch me. Everything had to come through Him first. The Word tells us that He is our refuge, our safe place, and our fortress. I had looked up the word fortress and found that it was an impenetrable or heavily protected building.

> *"I will say of the Lord, 'He is my refuge and my fortress, My God, in whom I trust [with great confidence, and on whom I rely]!'" Psalm 91:2*

I pictured Him all around me, almost like bubble wrap, only much more impenetrable. Anything that came toward me had to go through Him first. The bubble wrap was His love. Everything would pass through His love before it came to me. Sharp words or actions would be softened before they reached me. They would have no effect on me. I would not have to endure any of the pain. This is the belief I hold about God as my refuge and fortress. It is an amazing way to live. His name is my strong tower.

> *"The name of the Lord is a strong tower; The righteous runs to it and is safe and set on high [far above evil]." Proverbs 18:10*

One Bible translation says the righteous run into it and are safe. I pictured myself in Him, safe and protected. I am the righteous, and I live in His name. I speak His name often. I put it before me in many circumstances. I believe there is power and wisdom in His name, and I expect things to change at the mention of it.

Knowing God as my Fortress and my belief in the name of Jesus have caused so much fear to be cast out of my life. His love casts out all fear. I was dealing with situations with power and clarity (and I still am). I needed this in my life as I walked with my husband during this difficult season.

It was a Sunday morning, and I had stayed back from church with the baby, my tenth child. I couldn't go that morning the way things were between my husband and me. He was fine with going and taking the other nine kids. I was home, praying and asking the Lord what to do with the situation we were going through in our marriage and family. I was to the point that I didn't want my marriage anymore if it stayed like this. I knew divorce wasn't what God wanted for us, either. I had been asking God what to do up until this time, but I don't know if I had stopped to listen to His answer.

I decided to quiet myself and just listen. The only thing I heard—it was impressed upon me—was that I needed to pack my bag. I didn't want to pack my bag. After all, I had ten kids, and what would that look like? My response was, "Really, Lord, you're asking me to pack my bag?" I knew that was what I needed to do. It seemed contradictory to all I had been taught, but I wasn't divorcing. I was packing my bag. I knew the Lord would direct me from there. I was taking the step as He directed, kind of like Abraham when God told him to sacrifice Isaac. Abraham took the step of obedience, believing and trusting God.

This step of obedience makes me think about what I have been taught. Each of us can ask ourselves, "Is what I have been taught right, or is it just what my parents were taught or what the church I grew up in taught?" We can go about life doing the traditional things the traditional ways without even knowing the truth or why we are doing things a certain way. Look at this verse:

> *"You disregard and neglect the commandment of God, and cling [faithfully] to the tradition of men." Mark 7:8*

Is that what most of us have been doing for years—just walking in the tradition of men? Is that why we haven't gotten the results in our lives we are longing for? It is time to get curious with ourselves so we understand why we are doing what we are doing and actually study the Word so we know and do what it says. We can't just keep following someone else's interpretation.

Abraham could have thought, "This isn't God. He wouldn't ask me to kill my son." The key in Abraham's life was that he knew God well enough that he knew when it was God speaking. He walked with God. We must be people who walk with God, not just people who talk the talk. We must walk the walk.

When we finally come to the realization that what we have been doing isn't working and we must do something different to get the change, that is when the results happen. It's like the saying "Let go and let God." It can feel irresponsible or even rebellious to go against the ways of the world or the ways that seem reasonable or logical. It can seem like it's wrong when the church, pastor, or even family doesn't agree. We need to know our Shepherd's voice and not follow the voice of a stranger. Many of the ways we have been taught are just reasonable, sensible, or even religious. Is that the God of the Bible?

Look at what Moses did. He went back to the place where he could have been put to death for killing one of the servants. Does that seem like what God would want him to do from our religious teaching or natural mind?

How about Noah being asked to build a humongous boat in the middle of the desert? There had been no rain there ever. Do we think that God will ask us to do only the ordinary thing? Do we think that He will ask us to do only the things that everyone agrees with? No, we know that is not true. He is an extraordinary God. He wants to do more in our lives than we could ask or imagine. He's the God of the impossible. Can I ask you how many impossible things you have done in your lifetime? Most of us tend to want to stay safe. We want to stay comfortable. We must ask ourselves if we are living big enough. If our daily lives don't require God, are we living big enough?

> *"For with God nothing [is or ever] shall be impossible."*
> *Luke 1:37*

The question is: Will we believe Him and obey Him? Will we step out and make the uncomfortable choice in an impossible situation? No doubt it was scary to think about what packing my bags might lead to. But did I really know what it might lead to? It's our thoughts that create the drama around the circumstances. I couldn't think of what it might mean. I just had to do the act of packing my bag. It's called simple obedience. Just do this step and do it scared and sick to your stomach and shaking if needed. So, I did it scared, and none of those things happened that my mind could have gone to. Most of what we fear doesn't even happen; it's just assumptions.

My husband came home. We talked; he saw my bag. He asked what I was doing. I said I couldn't go on like that anymore, so I was going to leave for a bit. I didn't know where I was going to go except for a motel. I didn't know for how long, but I knew I wasn't leaving the kids. I also knew I wasn't divorcing him. I just needed some space and time to get out of the middle of our situation. I needed time and space to see it from a different perspective. Sometimes when a person is in the middle of things, it's hard to see the situation clearly. It can feel like you are drowning in it. I was taking a step out of the ordinary so our lives could change or shift. And they did. You know what happened next? He said, "No, you stay. I'll go."

We had an unfinished cabin about an hour out of town. He wanted to go out there for a few nights, and we agreed with that step. He packed his bag and left. I was in awe of how God worked it out so I didn't have to leave. He sees everything, and He knows our hearts. He is pleased with our obedience.

> *"Samuel said, "Has the Lord as great a delight in burnt offerings and sacrifices as in obedience to the voice of the Lord? Behold, to obey is better than sacrifice, and to heed [is better] than the fat of rams." 1 Samuel 15:22*

> *"And we know [with great confidence] that God [who is deeply concerned about us] causes all things to work together [as a plan] for good for those who love God, to those who are called according to His plan and purpose." Romans 8:28*

I know that because I love God, He worked out this situation for my good and the good of my husband. Did you see that it says, "all things"? As believers who love God, you and I can know that ALL things will work out for our good. Will you choose to believe this and walk in it?

My simple obedience brought the shift we needed in our marriage and family. Things continued to change for the better in our relationship. Justin came back after a few days. I had more confidence to do and say what God had put on my heart, knowing I was hearing from Him.

One thing I knew was that I wasn't doing life the same way anymore. I knew God didn't want me to do it the same way, either. Our lives had to change for His name's sake. I noticed that the more light I had in me, the less darkness could stay. That is why life was changing rapidly. Darkness was being exposed, and it had to flee.

God has set before us life and death. I picture it like Him putting out both hands, one with life in it and one with death in it. He says to choose life. That hand with life in it doesn't look any different on the outside, but when He opens it, we see the amazing abundant life He has for us. He says to go ahead and choose it. It won't disappoint. There is more here for you than you could dream or pray for.

It's your choice. Do you want your life to stay just the way it is? Or do you want to live the extraordinary, impossible life God has for you? Because I chose God's way, my marriage is thriving now, and it's ten times better than it was before. Because I chose God and His way, my children are moving forward and have so many more opportunities. If I wouldn't have done the scary thing and followed God's way by packing my bag, I don't know where we would be now. We probably wouldn't be married. Our family of ten children would have been split apart. There would have been so much division. Sometimes we think that by not saying anything, by not rocking the boat, we are saving our marriage, our children, or our job. That inactivity gets us nowhere and doesn't change anything. Being lukewarm is not pleasing to God. We are never not going anywhere. We are either going forward toward God or backward away from Him. Friend, stay in the forward motion. You won't be sorry.

What are we trying to save by doing nothing? We think we are keeping everyone safe. We think we are protecting everyone. Do we want our marriage or other areas of life to stay in an unhealthy place? Do we want our children to only see our marriage in an unhealthy state and not moving forward? If we are okay with an unhealthy situation, what are we saying to our kids? Why don't you be the one to turn the situation around with God's guidance? That attitude, issue, or problem that has been in your family for generations … why don't you be the one to take a step toward change? What if that step changed everything for future generations? Yes, it's that critical!

I'm glad I did the scary thing. I'm glad I did the different thing. I'm glad I did what God told me to do. What is your next step to shift the seemingly impossible situation or circumstance in your life? Ask God and then listen and do what He puts on your heart. He's with you and won't let you go. He's on your side. He's fighting for you. He works out all things for the good of those who love Him. Do you love Him? He delivers us from trouble. I encourage you, friend, to just obey.

YOUR NEXT STEPS JOURNALING

_____

_____

_____

_____

_____

_____

_____

_____

_____

_____

_____

_____

_____

_____

_____

_____

_____

_____

_____

_____

_____

_____

_____

CHAPTER 10

ON THE VERGE OF A GRAND MAL SEIZURE

During this season that my husband was spiraling into breakdown and depression, I wasn't feeling great either. Over the years, our family would go to a naturopath-type doctor about an hour from where we lived. We had gone to her for minor issues with a couple of our kids and me. I chose to go to her for myself because she was the closest professional who did natural medicine rather than prescription drugs. Since I was either pregnant or nursing for nineteen years, and I was not able to take pharmaceuticals for most of that time, we were thankful to have this option and were getting positive results with her expertise.

When I went in to see her for one particular appointment, she had me lie on the bed like usual. Then she proceeded to take my pulses. Yes, I learned then that we have more than one pulse. Next, she placed acupuncture needles in the spots where she would always put them. From our previous experience, I knew she would leave the room for about twenty minutes while those needles did their work. I just relaxed and lay still and quiet on the table as I was instructed.

When she finally came back, she said, "When you came in here, you were on the verge of a grand mal seizure." I can't remember what else she did during that appointment. She usually would send me home with some type of prescription, like eating nine grapes and half a cup of canned peas, or eating three slices of canned peaches and some pickled beets. The prescriptions were usually interesting combinations like that. Occasionally, she would also prescribe a supplement. At this point, I don't remember what she prescribed, if anything. She may have encouraged me to see another doctor.

As far as I can recall, I didn't go back to her. I'm pretty sure that shortly after that visit, she closed her practice due to an illness of her own, and I think I was pregnant with baby number ten somewhere around that time. I don't remember returning to her.

Back to the thought of me being on the verge of a grand mal seizure. I realized that I had been feeling spinny here and there. I was homeschooling and had nine or ten kids. Why wouldn't I feel spinny, right? In those days, I didn't have a lot of extra time to think about how I was feeling and what the cause would be. I was just doing life, taking care of one need at a time. When I paused to think about what was going on around me, I realized we were going through some difficult stuff. We had just switched churches and closed a business. We had situations going on with extended family, nine kids and a new baby, and more. I realized that the "storm" that was going on around me had gotten inside of me.

When I got home, I didn't go straight to a medical doctor. I remember briefly considering it. I asked God what He wanted me to do with the news. We had just learned about healing through our new church, and I was led to seek out God's healing in this illness and not go to a medical doctor.

I was determined to walk it out with God. I took in the information the naturopath had given me about my health. I pondered it, and I did not panic. I was not worried. I asked the Lord what to do. After all, He is my life, according to the Word, and I am led by Him.

"When Christ, who is our life, appears, then you also will appear with Him in glory." Colossians 3:4

"For all who are allowing themselves to be led by the Spirit of God are sons of God." Romans 8:14

I had nine or ten kids at home. I was homeschooling. I could have gone to a medical doctor, but that was not the way I was led. I was led to stay home and continue life as normal. If I felt the spinning sensation come on, I would let my older daughters know that I needed to go lie down for a bit. They would manage the household for me for about thirty minutes to an hour while I was lying on my bed.

As I lay down, I relaxed and completely cleared my mind, letting go of any worry or anxiety. I knew I had to stop any negative thoughts. You know those thoughts that continually swirl around in your mind? I could not let any fears in, or the spinning would grow worse.

Earlier, I mentioned the storm that I had let inside me. I had allowed my circumstances to get in me, and they had affected me physically.

I had to quiet the storm. I did this by letting go of all the negative thoughts. Instead, I focused on the Word. I knew I had to let go of all of it and completely lean on God. My mind needed rest. How often do we go over and over thoughts in our mind, trying to figure things out, trying to see where we went wrong, or blaming the other person—only to end up in the same spot? I was anxious, depressed, worried, resentful, stressed, offended, and bitter. I needed God's wisdom, His guidance, and His hand in my life.

Concerning certain circumstances, I would check my heart by asking myself questions. Am I just being unthankful? What did I do wrong? Why is this happening? The truth was my heart was right toward God. I loved Him. I wanted to do what was right.

I lay there on my bed, giving my life to God—all of it. I was yielding my mind to God. I spoke out, "No weapon formed against me shall prosper, and by Your stripes, I am healed."

> *"'No weapon that is formed against you will succeed; And every tongue that rises against you in judgment you will condemn. This [peace, righteousness, security, and triumph over opposition] is the heritage of the servants of the Lord, And this is their vindication from Me,' says the Lord."*
> *Isaiah 54:17*

> *"But He was wounded for our transgressions, He was crushed for our wickedness [our sin, our injustice, our wrongdoing]; The punishment [required] for our well-being fell on Him, And by His stripes (wounds) we are healed."*
> *Isaiah 53:5*

I would pray in the Spirit. Yes, in tongues, speaking to God and not to man. Edifying myself. Building myself up in my most holy faith. Praying in the Holy Spirit.

> *"For one who speaks in an unknown tongue does not speak to people but to God; for no one understands him or catches his meaning, but by the Spirit he speaks mysteries [secret truths, hidden things]."* *1 Corinthians 14:2*

> *"One who speaks in a tongue edifies himself; but one who prophecies edifies the church [promotes growth in spiritual wisdom, devotion, holiness, and joy]."* *1 Corinthians 14:4*

"But you, beloved, build yourselves up on [the foundation of] your most holy faith [continually progress, rise like and edifice higher and higher], pray in the Holy Spirit." Jude 1:20

When we pray in the Spirit, we rise up like a towering building, standing firm and tall on the foundation of the Word of God. I was so thankful for this way to pray. I believed with all my heart that I was praying out mysteries of healing and other things as I lay down on my bed and let His presence consume me. What if I didn't believe it was working? I'll tell you that if I wouldn't have believed it was working, it probably wouldn't have worked. We receive the promises by faith.

"So that you will not be [spiritually] sluggish, but [will instead be] imitators of those who through faith [lean on God with absolute trust and confidence in Him and in His power] and by patient endurance [even when suffering] are [now] inheriting the promises." Hebrews 6:12

After a couple of weeks of the routine of lying down, praying, and quoting scripture, I no longer had to lie down when I felt the spinning come on. I still had a little spinning here and there, but it wasn't enough to cause me to have to lie down. The Lord had healed me by faith in

His Word. He healed me by His hand and by me choosing to believe and have faith in the Word for my circumstances. I love the verse:

"Bless and affectionately praise the Lord, O my soul, And do not forget any of His benefits; Who forgives all your sins, Who heals all your diseases." Psalm 103:2–3

For so many years, I believed by faith that I was forgiven. I did not know anything about the healing power of God. Now when I see the benefit of forgiveness and the benefit of healing in the same verse, I am in awe of how so many churches only believe in the forgiveness of sin. At least that seems to be their main focus. They don't seem to pay any attention to the fact that in the same verse, it says that He heals all of our diseases.

People say, "Well, look at all the sick believers," or "I prayed and prayed for people to be healed, and I don't see it; therefore, God must not want to heal us," or "He will heal someone if it's His will." The question is: Do they believe God will heal when they ask Him to? Do they have the faith for healing? Remember the story about the woman who had suffered bleeding for twelve years and could find no cure? She came up to Jesus and touched the fringe on His robe, believing that she would be healed. Jesus felt the healing power go out of Him. He said that her faith had made her well.

"He said to her, 'Daughter, your faith [your personal trust and confidence in Me] has made you well. Go in peace (untroubled, undisturbed well-being).'" Luke 8:48

My thought is: Do we see forgiveness? I mean actually, physically see it? No, not really. We may see a changed life, but we don't physically see forgiveness. We just believe that we are forgiven. We believe by faith, right? So, it's the same idea with healing. We believe we have healing by faith. Just because we don't see the healing immediately doesn't mean we don't have it or that God doesn't heal. It can take time for the healing to manifest. It can take time for us to gain faith in this truth, especially when we have been taught against it for so many years. We can even lose faith in it before it manifests in our lives.

I want to share a couple of other healing stories from my own life—stories that have made me a solid believer in healing. One warm summer day, I was doing my normal daily chores, and the kids were playing outside. I think I had ten of them at the time. My little guy Blaize, he was two at the time, came running up to me in bare feet, whimpering. He wanted to show me his foot. I stopped what I was doing and looked at the bottoms of his feet. I noticed that behind each toe, in the crease of one of the joints, there were little open cracks. I could see that they would have been a bit painful.

I was feeling weary over all the needs of the children and our home. I was learning to rely on God. It was the same season my husband was struggling with burnout. My first response was now to speak out the words "In Jesus' name." So, I touched Blaize's foot and said, "In Jesus' name," believing in its power. I thanked the Lord for healing those little toes. My eyes tear up even now as I tell this story. God's love for me is so evident, being His daughter, during a time when I was so desperate for His help and leaning on Him alone, and He came through. He so specifically and lovingly answered my cry for help.

Just pause a moment, friend. Feel that love of the Father surround you in your moment of need and manifest in your life in such a tangible way. I wish I could hear every story of what He has done in your life as you pause right now. I know I will find out one day in heaven.

I prayed, believing, over those toes. Just as quick as my little guy came running to me whimpering and disturbed about the pain on the bottom of his feet, he ran off to play again after our short but valuable encounter. I knew at that point that if I tried to reel him back in and bandage his toes and try to put socks and shoes on him, it wouldn't have worked very well for two reasons. First, he was having fun playing in the water and grass. He would not have stood for it for a second to have me doctoring his feet while he wanted to go play. Second, the bandages, socks, and shoes wouldn't have stayed on for more than two seconds. You know how kids don't want to deal with shoes, especially where water is involved. I decided to let him play and figured I would check his feet at bedtime and do what was needed, if anything, at that time. I had prayed, believing. Taking care of them before bed would give him a whole night to keep the ointment and bandages on and give those little cracks a good chance to heal.

Well, when I checked on them that night, I didn't see one crack. God had so lovingly healed my little boy's feet. I felt so loved because He had heard me, an overwhelmed mom's cry for help. He not only heard me, but He also answered me. It was such a simple prayer of belief in His name. Sometimes we complicate things, don't we? But it can be as simple as asking and believing.

After all, in the Gospels, the disciples asked Jesus what they needed to do in order to do the works of God.

> *"Then they asked Him, 'What are we to do, so that we may habitually be doing the works of God?' Jesus answered, 'This is the work of God: that you believe [adhere to, trust in, rely on, and have faith] in the One whom He has sent.'" John 6:28–29*

He sent Jesus, and according to the Word, Jesus is the Word.

> *"In the beginning [before all time] was the Word (Christ), and the Word was with God, and the Word was God Himself." John 1:1*

> *"And the Word (Christ) became flesh, and lived among us; and we [actually] saw His glory, glory as belongs to the [One and] only begotten Son of the Father, [the Son who is truly unique, the only One of His kind, who is] full of grace and truth (absolutely free of deception)." John 1:14*

This means that our work as believers is to believe the Word and believe in the Holy Spirit. It's really that simple. I remember asking God what He wanted me to do as a believer. Our lives are filled with so many opportunities, acts of service, and good works with family, friends, and strangers. I needed Him to simplify it for me. This is what He said: Believe the Word and my Spirit.

Here's another healing story: I had just had my tenth baby, and the doctor had just come in to check me before I was discharged to go home. By this time, the doctors pretty much just asked how I was. I was a "professional" at having babies by the tenth one, right? I remember saying, "I'm good. Everything's going well."

I had become a very positive thinker by this time. I rarely paid attention to anything negative. My thinking had also become very scriptural. I remember one time when I was talking to one of my teenage sons (Logen), and he was telling me that he was letting a friend borrow his cell phone at a game. His friend was saying that he thought his parents were "in service." By the way, his parents were pastors. At that time, our family went to nearly every church service that was available. So, I said, "I wonder what service they are in?" My son rolled his eyes and said in an irritated voice, "Mom, he was talking about cell service. Why do you have to think so biblically all the time?" I laughed and laughed. "I'll take that as a compliment," I responded. As I'm writing this, I'm laughing so hard I have tears streaming down my face.

It's amazing what kids say sometimes. They often say the truth.

Let's go back to the childbirth healing story. The doctor congratulated us and discharged us from the hospital. We got home and were getting things situated, hugging all the kids, letting them greet their new sister, and settling in for the night. I would normally be discharged right after supper so I wouldn't have to deal with a meal when I got home.

Before long, we were all heading to bed. In the middle of the night, I tried to get up with the baby, and I could barely walk. A small area was very tender on my left upper calf. It was growing extremely sore, red, warm, and hard … I realized this as I limped to the bathroom. I asked my husband to get the baby because it was painful for me to step down with that leg. I didn't feel like I should hold the baby and walk at the same time; that is how unstable I felt. I was thinking and asking the Lord what was going on with my leg. I realized it was a blood clot. I had never had one before, but I had heard them described, and this was obviously a blood clot.

Right away, I said, "In Jesus' name" and asked the Lord what I should do about it. I had made it a habit to go to

Him first with things in my life. I listened and felt like I was okay not going to the doctor for a few days. The plan was to pray over it in the Spirit and say and believe those verses; no weapon formed against me shall prosper, and by Your stripes, I am healed.

I also searched Google for how to naturally thin blood. I wasn't against going to the doctor, but this is the way I felt led. I told my husband that I didn't want to be foolish. I knew this was serious, but I also knew I didn't want to be put on blood thinners and have to stop nursing my baby if I didn't have to. From Google, I learned that I could make a concoction of natural ingredients and drink a cup of it at least four times a day. I believed God and drank the concoction for two to three days. By the end of that time, the clot was thinned and completely dissolved.

> *"See what an incredible quality of love the Father has shown to us, that we would [be permitted to] be named and called and counted the children of God! And so we are! For this reason the world does not know us, because it did not know Him." 1 John 3:1*

The NIV version says: "See what great love the Father has lavished on us, that we should be called the children of God!" How loved I felt and still feel. God listens, cares, answers, and heals. He pays attention to every detail of our lives. Why not let Him into every area? It takes yielding one area at a time. It takes believing Him over what we see. He is faithful. Will you believe you are healed?

MOVING FORWARD JOURNALING

_____

_____

_____

_____

_____

_____

_____

_____

_____

_____

_____

_____

_____

_____

_____

_____

_____

_____

_____

_____

_____

CHAPTER 11

STRIPPED OF WHO I WAS

Without even being aware of it until we had to find out the hard way, my husband and I were people-pleasers. I started out that way, and that was all I ever knew. It's what I was exposed to growing up. We continued going down that road, not even recognizing the unhealthy and destructive place it would lead us to.

We had four kids when we moved back to the small town where I had grown up until I was fifteen. My husband moved there with his family when he was sixteen. We both had moved away from there years before, and now we were moving back, married and with a family. His parents still lived in that town, plus a few other relatives lived there.

We moved back to take over the greenhouse business that his parents had operated for several years. They were ready to sell it and pass it on if we wanted to take it over. We were excited to live near them and start this new adventure with our own business. Now, as I share about this situation that arose, I in no way want to put down or speak against anyone. I'm just sharing this situation for the purpose of encouraging others who find themselves in a similar place.

The healing power of God is so transparent in this story I am about to share. I am in awe of God and His goodness in our lives. His restoration power concerning offense, bitterness, and a broken heart brings me so much gratitude for Him.

Once we moved to Miles City, this whole drama started. So many beautiful events happened during this time, as well as extremely difficult events.

My in-laws are beautiful, caring, generous people. They seemed to love me very much, saying that they "couldn't have handpicked me for their son better themselves." They adored their only son, the only redhead in the family for generations, "except for grandpa's red beard." Justin was also the baby of the family. He had achieved great honors in sports and has always been a handsome, great guy all around.

It became evident shortly after we moved there that they wanted to spend a lot of time with us. They worked in the greenhouse, mostly voluntarily, and often enjoyed stopping by our house. The greenhouse business was located on the same property as our residence. One or both of them would swing by as many as one to three times a day. Most of the time, they were saying hi and dropping off household items such as chairs, towels, and plates, just to name a few. They also brought food such as boxes of ripe bananas and bags of flour and sugar—to make banana bread, of course. I would get a call from my father-in-law, telling me that he had a plan for his granddaughters and me to make banana bread for him. After all, the girls need something to do, right? Along with that, they dropped off clothes, saying, "I heard my grandson needed some socks," or "This shirt didn't fit me; will it work for any of you?" The list went on, and they continued to call or stop by.

My husband's dad was the youngest in a family of thirteen children. I am sure that gave him a different view of life compared to the way most of us grew up. My heart was to honor them. The Bible tells us to honor our parents. That is what I wanted to do, but it seemed like it was getting harder and harder as the days went by.

I often wrestled with thoughts like "Why am I not being thankful for the things they are bringing?" and "Why am I not wanting them around?" I tried setting up a plan of having dinner with them once a week, every Sunday. That didn't work because we had already seen them every day that week. So then, I didn't want to plan a get-together.

My husband was dealing with his own frustrations with his parents in the business, so you are only hearing my side and what I was dealing with from home. I believe my husband and I were both frustrated with the intrusion of his parents, but we didn't know what to do. We felt as though we weren't listened to when we did try to discuss it. Obviously, we all had a lot to learn.

They were literally at our house one to three times a day for eleven years unless either family was out of town, but then there would always be a phone call. If we would go to their house in the evening for a dinner invite, my mother-in-law would usually call ahead of time and tell me to bring the baby's pajamas so she could give the baby a bath. This was a sweet gesture. At times, I thought it was helpful, but after a season, it began to feel intrusive rather than helpful.

At one time, my mother-in-law offered to bring lunch to my husband, her son, at work. This was also a kind gesture. But he was already working overtime, so if he ate lunch at work, that meant he wouldn't come home at lunchtime. Remember, our house was on the same property as our business. The kids and I needed to have their father, my husband, interrupt our day. It helped when he showed his presence in the home at lunchtime. I'm sure most moms can relate to that.

I mentioned to my husband not to have his mom bring him lunch, and I believe I also mentioned it to her. It felt like we were constantly asking them to stop doing things. Sometimes, they listened; sometimes, they didn't; and sometimes, we didn't even voice our needs.

Another situation that often came up was if Justin, the kids, or I said anything about needing something, it miraculously would show up on the kitchen counter the next day or be at their house the next time we visited. I thought, *Why don't I appreciate that, Mom of five, six, seven … kids?*

I wrestled with these thoughts for years. I wanted to appreciate all the giving and visiting, but I felt intruded on and like my positions as a mom and a wife were being taken over.

My husband was stressed out, working around the clock and trying to meet the needs of his family. We would try to relax on a Sunday afternoon, and there would be a knock at the door. It would be one or both of his parents wanting to drop something off again or say hi. As much as we love them, it was too much.

There came a time when I knew I couldn't live this way anymore. Something had to change. I didn't enjoy confrontation, but I knew I had to change the situation for the sake of my family and our future relationship with my in-laws. I felt stripped of who I was as a mom of nine kids and as a wife.

I was homeschooling and felt like I had constant interruptions during the day. I would be working with the kids, and there would be a knock at the door. Most of the time, it was one of my in-laws just popping in. Any parent or teacher knows how long it can take to get everyone sitting and working on their schoolwork or chores. Again, my heart was to honor them, but honor can quickly become people-pleasing if we continue to say it's okay when it really isn't. I felt that I wasn't clear on what was and wasn't okay in this situation. I knew I was uncomfortable with all the unannounced visits, but I wasn't sure if what I was feeling was right. I didn't want to be selfish or unthankful or unloving. I didn't know how to listen to myself or God. This created a lot of torment inside me around the situation.

Finally, my husband and I agreed to go and talk to his parents. We laid out what we needed to change and what wasn't working. It was a peaceful conversation, but it became clear that his mom thought I was against her.

So many of the issues we faced were because of a lack of clear communication. If we can recognize that both parties were coming from two different backgrounds, then we can process the situation from our experience and exposure from the past and try to move forward with understanding and compromise.

Little changed after that conversation. The entanglement was tight between them and us. It felt to me like they had a hold on my family and me and wouldn't let go. We sent a couple of text messages to try to communicate what we wanted to change because the conversations had not brought about the change that was needed at that point.

After a couple of months, I went back over to their house. This time, I went by myself to talk to my mother-in-law. I told her that we needed a six-month break from them. My husband couldn't deal with the situation, as he was going into a breakdown. I knew I had to do something to save my family. If we ever wanted to have a healthy relationship with them, I had to do something to change what was going on.

I said, "Don't come over; don't call. We need a break to work things out in our own family as well as with you guys." She responded, "Well, we can just see Justin and the kids and not you." I said, "No, we aren't doing things that way. We're serious about the six-month break."

You might be asking yourself what we did about birthdays, Christmas, and other events that came up during that time. Yes, there were so many events of theirs that we didn't attend, and events of ours that they didn't attend, but it had to happen. It couldn't go on as it had. It wasn't worth continuing all the birthday gatherings and showing up at our events together just to say we did it. It was important for us to give the space needed for all of us to grow and change what needed to be changed. Why keep interacting in an unhealthy way? It won't get better on its own. If we hadn't done something, I'm not sure where the relationship would be today.

During those six months and quite a while longer, I would find myself looking toward the front door of our house: the place where one or both of them would show up one to three times a day. My anxiety would rise, and I would tell myself that we weren't in that season anymore. I didn't realize the stress or anxiety I had allowed with that situation. It was deep, but as time went on, it got less and less.

I asked the Lord to counsel me through the feelings of being stripped of who I was. I knew I couldn't live with that pain. He showed me that I was as unhealthy as they were because I allowed the intrusion. This thought helped me let go of any bitterness or resentment that was trying to creep in.

My heart was broken at the thought that some years were taken from me with my kids and my husband. The Lord showed me that I had been there with my family all along, and not all the times with his parents were bad. I asked God to do in my life what the Word said in the Psalms.

"He heals the brokenhearted and binds up their wounds [healing their pain and comforting their sorrow]." Psalm 147:3

I asked Him to heal my broken heart and bind up my wounds. Whenever I would feel the pain of the situation, I would thank Him for healing my broken heart and binding up my wounds. After a couple of weeks, I no longer felt the pain of being stripped of who I was. He healed my broken heart. I'm so grateful. I'm so loved by Him. He's so good.

God also gave me this verse during this season:

"Beloved, never avenge yourselves, but leave the way open for God's wrath [and His judicial righteousness]; for it is written [in Scripture], "VENGEANCE IS MINE, I WILL REPAY," says the Lord." Romans 12:19

This means that God will pay us back for everything the devil has taken from us. The word repay or recompense means to make amends to (someone) for loss or harm suffered and to compensate them.

This verse gave me so much hope and joy. I believed it with all my heart, and I still do. There's no longer any lack in my life. I fully expect repayment and abundance to overflow in my life. The feeling of being stripped of who I am as a wife and a mom is completely gone. God has completely recompensated me for all the loss and harm I suffered in my life. For this, I am forever grateful to my Heavenly Father. Without this healing in my life, I can only imagine the pain and bitterness I would be living with.

I chose to pray for my in-laws. This is the prayer I would pray:

> *"Father, bless my in-laws. I may not understand why they did what they did, but that is between them and You. I pray that You will give them divine guidance in every area of their lives. Lord, make them a blessing to others."*

I would pray this instead of thinking negative thoughts about them. I knew they were good people, and I knew that God had used them to be a blessing in the lives of many people. Even though I wasn't seeing them as a blessing in my life at that time, I wanted God to bless them. I also wanted to have a restored relationship with them. I didn't want to sever the relationship for good. Grandparents are important to children, and they were important to us. I knew that one day, I would be a mother-in-law and grandparent. I wanted to treat them the way I would want to be treated. So much growth and purpose had to take place during this season so that my husband, my children, and I could relate well with them again.

I had to renew my mind with the Word and believe it over my circumstances. I had to choose not to blame and not to be bitter or angry or resentful. I chose to see where I was wrong and to change myself. I chose to leave the unhealthy spot, not knowing how my husband, my children, or his parents would respond. I'm so thankful I did the hard thing. Now, we have a relationship with his parents, and it's healthy. I have my children, and I have a relationship with all of them, and it's healthy. I have a relationship with my husband, and it's healthy and growing. Life would not have turned out this way if I wouldn't have obeyed what God was saying.

Is there an area of your life that you need to step out of? What do you need to change? Changing yourself is key. Don't stay in an unhealthy spot just because you don't want to hurt anyone. In the long run, there is so much more hurt and destruction if you continue in an unhealthy way. Your children are watching. What if they see you take a stand against unrighteousness? What if they see you speak up and use your voice? Could this keep them from having some of the same troubles in their lives? What if you are changing in a positive way for the generations ahead? Isn't it worth being uncomfortable for a little while to bring about right relationships in the future?

I am so glad I did the hard thing a few years ago. Now we can enjoy all the relationships coming into our large family, and there will be many sons-in-law and daughters-in-law as well as grandchildren to love and enjoy. I'm thankful we demonstrated healthy communication and stepped out of people-pleasing for the generations ahead and for the sake of righteousness.

YOUR NEXT STEPS JOURNALING

_____

_____

_____

_____

_____

_____

_____

_____

_____

_____

_____

_____

_____

_____

_____

_____

_____

_____

_____

_____

_____

_____

_____

_____

_____

CHAPTER 12

BACK TO SCHOOL

During the season of my husband's depression, he continued to be discontent with where he was in work and life. At one point, these words came out of my mouth: Why don't we move and go to a Bible school? I was shocked that I said it, but the thought was obviously in my mind, and my husband needed a shift in life. My thought was that if he wasn't happy here, maybe he would be happy somewhere else. No matter what, it was obvious that something needed to change. We couldn't go on much longer the way we were.

I was interested in going to a school down south. I had that desire on my heart but had not spoken it out loud yet. I didn't quite believe it was possible. After all, we had nine kids at home and lived way up in Montana. How would it go to move and start school and work in another place? I knew anything was possible with God. Besides doing what God called me to do, I wanted my husband to find himself and his vision for his life again.

We decided to take a trip down to visit the college. We would look at houses and the surrounding area and check out the school. It was one of those preview weekends. One son was planning to go in that direction in the fall anyway. Another daughter wasn't sure of her next step, and two more kids were close enough to finishing high school that it wouldn't hurt them to see it also.

Off we went, leaving our five younger kids at home with the oldest sister, Jayna, and her husband. (They are such a blessing and an amazing couple.) We made a twenty-hour drive traveling with six of us in our twelve-passenger van. We had four drivers in the car, and our plan was to drive straight through. Four of us would drive five hours apiece. My husband would take the last five hours of the trip, which would take place during the wee hours of the morning. It was a memorable trip. Lots of bonding took place during this road trip with this many bodies in one car for twenty hours.

We finally pulled in early in the morning. The hotel room was smaller than we expected. It had two queen beds and a pullout couch, without much more space than that. I'm pretty sure one child decided the floor would be better than sleeping with the sibling.

I'd learned over the years that I wouldn't add to the drama, so I just said, "Whatever you decide," and went to bed.

I enjoyed checking out the area, getting to know the college, meeting amazing people, looking at potential houses for us to buy, and imagining living there and all that would entail. We looked at the schools and saw the grocery stores. We checked out the church and visited a possible daycare.

As we spent hours looking at houses, we ended the day not finding one that would fit us, a family of eleven. We looked at each place, trying to picture us living there. Not one of them was a close enough match. My husband kept seeing the tornado shelters in the garage. First, he thought it was a cool place to change oil or something like that.

When he found out they were tornado shelters, his interest in moving there diminished even more.

At that point in my life, I could have lived anywhere. I had such peace with God and myself. I knew I was to put my kids in school and attend Bible school. Those were the directions I had received from my Heavenly Father.

Well, long story short, we went back to Montana, and we did not move the family. Our oldest son, Luke, started at that Bible college the next fall. As soon as we returned home, we got the news that our church would be starting its first year of a Bible Institute in the fall. That settled it. I would be going at my church in my own town that fall. My husband also got word right when we returned that he had earned a promotion at work. That settled his discontentment with his job in town, at least for a little while longer.

In that season, our bank account was low, and our finances had been extremely tight for a couple of years. For me, it was by faith that I was going to Bible school. It would cost a few thousand dollars per year, and it would be a two-year program. I had no idea how God would provide, but I knew He would see me through what He called me to do. I just kept saying, "I'm going to

Bible school" and thanking the Lord for the provision for it. Here's how it went:

It was early August, and the bills were piling up. The tuition for Bible school was due at the end of August. Let me tell you what happened starting in June of that same summer. Toward the end of June, our refrigerator went out in our kitchen. We had an older one in the laundry room, so we weren't completely without one, but we were also used to using two of them.

Right away when this fridge went out, my husband said, "I'm going to go get my tools." What rose up on the inside of me was so unexpected that I put my hand over my mouth. I couldn't believe I said "No!" so boldly. Now, I didn't really care about getting a new fridge. I also didn't care about getting old things fixed.

What I did care about was my husband. He had been on overload, fixing all the things at the house and trying to make everything work. Not only work so we could continue daily functions as usual but also trying to make it all work financially. He was sinking deeper and deeper into stress, anxiety, and depression. When these words rose up in me—"No, don't fix it"—I knew it was the Spirit of God speaking through me.

This refrigerator was about fifteen years old. Some of the shelving on the inside of the door was breaking. There was no need to fix it; it had seen its day, and we had gotten full use out of it. I did not believe God wanted us to continue fixing this broken-down fridge. My husband looked at me and said, "Okay." I was leaving to go to a baseball game, and when I got there, I called my husband and said, "If you really feel like we need to fix the fridge, go ahead." I left it at that.

We ended up pulling out the fridge and getting rid of it. The space in our kitchen sat empty for just over two weeks. We used the older extra fridge in our laundry room. No, it wasn't convenient, but it served its purpose for a short season as our main refrigerator. Every time I walked by that empty space in our kitchen, I thanked the Lord for the fridge that would fit there.

One day, my husband called me and said, "Go pick out your new refrigerator." I reluctantly said, "Okay." I knew we didn't really have the money. I decided ahead of time that I would choose the fridge that would fit that spot and be exactly what I wanted. Off I went to the appliance store following my husband's direction. I asked if they had any sales going on. They showed me what was on sale. I wasn't going to go smaller, and I wasn't going to go with the color I didn't want just because it was cheaper. I was going to pick the one that I wanted in our kitchen as we moved forward. It ended up with only one fridge that fit the spot just right. We needed one with double doors. The ones with big doors would hit our island when it was open, causing the door not to open all the way and not allowing the vegetable drawer to open.

I picked it out and told the lady we would call her when we wanted it delivered. A couple of weeks went by. Then one day, my husband called me and told me that he was having the new refrigerator delivered on Friday. Well, at this particular store, we had an account, so we put it on our account. The fridge was delivered. We didn't want to load up our accounts at this time. We were taking the steps; I was trusting that God was leading us.

We got the fridge and went about believing God. We thanked Him for the fridge and for the money to pay the bill. It was now early- to mid-July.

We had also been dealing with a leak in our roof for a while. My husband had fixed it himself and also called trusted professionals to fix it. It still leaked. He had torn out the drywall and insulation to watch the leak, and that area was open for about a year. He was trying to get to the bottom of where this leak was coming from. At one point, he thought it was stopped and closed up the wall. He had it all put together and found that it was leaking again. It would not stop.

You can imagine his frustration. I was watching all this and trusting God. We had done all we knew to fix the leak. It wasn't worth getting upset about. I knew God wanted it fixed for us. One day, I said, "I'm not paying attention to that anymore. God's got this." Every time I walked by that open space in our living area, I thanked God for taking care of it. I knew if we needed to do anything else about it, He would show us. I thanked the Lord that it was fixed before it happened.

By now, it was the beginning of August, and bills were piling up. Remember, I was planning to start Bible school at the end of the month. We had a new refrigerator to pay for. The normal monthly bills were coming due, and there was no extra money in sight. I was just speaking and believing God that I would start school and all the bills would be taken care of.

We got to the middle of August, and a hailstorm came through our community. One of the pieces of hail went through the skylight in our roof and hit the floor of our den. It was a golf ball size hailstorm. That was the only visible damage we could see. We knew we would need to call insurance to file a claim on this incident and look at the rest of the roof on our property. We made the call, and an insurance adjuster came out to look at the damage. After assessing our property, he informed us that the whole roof would need to be replaced.

Do you see how God fixed our leak? It didn't happen how I would have expected, but it happened. The insurance adjuster also told us that all of our garage doors needed to be changed as well. Both my husband and I told him that most of the dents in the garage doors were from our kids, not the hailstorm. Neither of us knew the other had mentioned this to him, but we found out later as we were conversing about it. The adjuster responded with, "Nope, all new garage doors as well."

I picked out wood-looking garage doors with windows at the top and handles to make it look like they were doors that could be opened that way. We were unable to find someone to roof our house because so many people in the area had hail damage and were needing new roofs that all of the roofers were scheduled way out. My husband recruited some helpers, and we ended up reroofing most of the house ourselves.

The roof we picked wasn't just any normal roof. We chose to put on a metal roof that was copper in color. It was more than I could have asked for. Everything just worked out. It wasn't hard. I knew the copper color was on my heart, but I didn't need the copper color. I just asked God if it would work out to get that color, and it did.

Reroofing the house ourselves allowed us to save some of the money and use it for other things. Every bill was paid in full that month, including the new refrigerator. Two days before I needed to have the first payment in for Bible school, I was able to pay in full. That same year, I put my youngest daughter, Evangelia, in daycare. She was the only one out of my ten children who ever went to daycare. Every week, I had the money to pay for daycare so I could go to Bible school.

You can imagine the joy I felt when I saw how God answered my prayers and met all our needs. He gave me the desires of my heart. It's in relationship, not religion, that the promises of God become ours. The copper metal roof, the new garage doors that I hadn't even asked for, Bible school paid in full, the refrigerator paid for, all of our bills that were stacking up, paid ... All this reminds me of a verse that I walk in and believe:

"Now to Him who is able to [carry out His purpose and] do superabundantly more than all that we dare ask or think [infinitely beyond our greatest prayers, hopes or dreams], according to His power that is at work within us." Ephesians 3:20

He did far more than I could ask or imagine. We had plenty of money for all the things we needed to pay for at that time. If I had to figure out how it would all work, I would have said, "It won't work." I have learned and I believe that with God, all things are possible.

"But Jesus looked at them and said, 'With people [as far as it depends on them] it is impossible, but with God all things are possible.'" Matthew 19:26

I have learned that I don't need to try to figure anything out. It's my job to trust and believe. I was totally relying on Him and trusting Him. As this verse says, for me, to live is Christ:

"For to me, to live is Christ [He is my source of joy, my reason to live] and to die is gain [for I will be with Him in eternity]." Philippians 1:21

The Word tells us He is our life. That's how I want to live—completely yielded to Him. I used to say the word "surrendered" instead of "yielded," but then I learned that surrender is what you do when you cease resistance to an enemy or opponent and submit to their authority. To yield means to relinquish one's possession of something, such as a position of advantage or point of superiority. This means I let go of the possession of my life and give it over to God. He is in the driver's seat. I want to be where He wants me, doing what He wants me to do.

> *"When Christ, who is our life, appears, then you also will appear with Him in glory." Colossians 3:4*

> *"You were bought with a price [you were actually purchased with the precious blood of Jesus and made His own]. So then, honor and glorify God with your body." 1 Corinthians 6:20*

What He leads me to, He will lead me through. I was bought with a price. I am not my own; I live in Him. I am hidden in Him. I am alive to God and dead to sin.

> *"Even so, consider yourselves to be dead to sin [and your relationship to it broken], but alive to God [in unbroken fellowship with Him] in Christ Jesus." Roman 6:11*

That summer, I remember talking to the Lord about continuing homeschooling. I knew I needed new strength, energy, and creativity to be able to continue strong. At that point, my youngest was only three years old. It would be another fifteen years of homeschooling if I were to graduate all of them that way.

Our lives had changed from when we started our homeschool journey. We no longer had a family business where the children could help with the work. My husband could not take them to work with him as often. It was especially important for our older children to get out of the house and get some experience on the job with their dad. We found that during the junior high and high school years, the youth needed other options than just being home all week with their mom.

It became clear to me the week before public school started that I needed to start transitioning the children into school. First, two of the elementary-age children would be starting school that fall, but as I was walking through the process of registering them, I knew the third one also needed to be enrolled. The Lord impressed it so heavily on my heart to send the third one. So I did.

I scheduled a time to go out with the three children to look at the school. They were nervous, excited, and scared. I was nervous, excited, scared, and determined. As I brought the three elementary-aged children out to the school to check it out, the Lord spoke to me. I was in our twelve-passenger van with them, heading to the school and telling God I needed Him to go with us. I told Him I was scared and I was only doing this because I was obeying His leading. I heard Him say so clearly, "They will excel and be a light." Such peace came over me at that moment. It dawned on me that that was why my children needed to go to school. They were to be a light, and they would do well; they would excel in school. From that point on, I knew without a doubt that God was leading this decision. I was standing on His Word.

The reasons it was so hard to put them in school were because homeschooling was all we had known with our family. Homeschooling is a lifestyle. Our days were scheduled so that everyone had their chores, and the older ones would help the younger ones. We didn't do specific testing with the school system; it was optional in our state, so we had opted out of all that. I didn't know where the children were with their education compared to their grades in the public schools. With homeschooling, if they didn't get a concept one year, they would get it the next. We were now leaving that familiar way and going into a foreign place, at least it was foreign to our family.

That same year, I would still have two junior-high-age kids at home, plus two preschoolers. We specifically worked toward preparing them to enter the public school system the following year. One would be going into the eighth grade and the other a freshman in high school.

I would be lying if I said it was easy. They were willing to go to school and play sports and do activities, but it was a total shift in our family's lifestyle. From the chores and meal routines to the way we ran our family, everything was changing. We went from everyone being home most of the time to everyone being gone most of the day. I started Bible school the same year that I started the two teens in school. My kindergartener also started that year. My tenth child went into a daycare—the first one from our family to be in that setting. What was I doing, you may ask? I was following God, I was doing it uncomfortable and scared, but I was doing it with trust and strength as well. I had seen God do so much in my life already that I could trust Him with this too.

By February of that school year, my husband got a job and would be leaving to work out of town eight days on and six days off.

Let me recap this year: 1. I started Bible school. 2. We switched the three children from the country school to the public schools in town. 3. We put the youngest one in daycare. 4. The ninth one started Kindergarten. 5. We had a daughter in the junior high school. 5. We had a son in the high school. 6. My husband left about mid-year to work out of town; he was gone more than he was home for one and a half years.

What a wild year! We had six different schools going that year, and we let some of the children start participating in sports. Of course, that means practices after school and games in the evenings and on the weekends. The children were beginning and finishing activities, so their schedules were constantly changing.

The other schedule that kept changing was my husband's. He was coming home and leaving again. I feel for all the families who do that for years. We live near the oil fields of North Dakota, and so many husbands from our town travel and work out of town. It was interesting trying to get used to my husband's schedule. I don't know if we ever really got used to it. It was just the way it was for that season. It would feel like a vacation when he came home. The chore routines would slack. The children would be excited and want to stay up or be with Dad for the day, but they had school. Then we would catch up and keep a pretty rigid routine while he was gone just so we could all survive. I was in the role of a single parent half the time for a year and a half. I think in these instances I just chose to be okay with being uncomfortable. I knew God was with me, and that's what I clung to.

All this was not an easy shift for the seven kids still at home, myself, or my husband. There were lots of tears, questions about schoolwork, time spent missing Dad, changes to the schedule, being the taxi driver to and from sporting events and practices, and quick meals. I would talk with my husband in the evening. He was doing well but didn't like being away from the family. He was learning so many new things, but it was a challenging season for him. Working in the oil fields is a different life. He stayed in a trailer house in the company's yard by the shop. He had his own room but shared the space with a couple of other guys. It was tough for him, knowing his family was back home. He struggled with the thought of why he was there and not with us.

I knew, on the other hand, why he was gone. He needed a refreshing; remember when he had gone through a low time? We needed to be apart for a bit to restore our marriage. The children needed to miss him and want him to come home. This time apart, it happened for all of us. We've all heard that "absence makes the heart grow fonder." In our family's case, we all needed to restore that fondness so we could move forward healthfully. Isn't God so good? The way He worked this was such a kind way to bring us back together as a family. I am so in awe of His amazing, gentle ways. Thank you so much, God! My love for Him is so great, and His love for me overwhelms me.

One morning, when I still had the express van and my husband had not left to work out of town yet, I went to drop off the kids at school. When I pulled up to the elementary school, my son, who had just started kindergarten and was the last of my children to be dropped off that day, was not wanting to go to school. He crawled under the very back seat of the twelve-passenger van. He was crying and screaming, "I don't want to go, I don't want to go." I got out, opened the side door, and calmly tried to persuade him to get out and go have a great day. He was not for it. He wanted nothing to do with it. The more I tried to persuade him, the louder he screamed. Rather than causing a scene, I closed the door and drove home with him still under the back seat. He became quiet then, knowing we were headed away from the school. My husband happened to be home. It was his off week. We talked with our son, spanked him, and both of us together brought him back to school just a little late. I remember my husband saying, "Okay, go ahead and take him back now," but I knew I would not be taking him back alone. I responded with, "Nope, you're coming with me this time."

I tell this story because, even as a seasoned parent (this happened with my ninth child), unexpected things happen. I have learned to be honest, like I was with my husband that day. I had done a lot of things alone concerning my children and wasn't about to continue the same way. I was changing. It's smart to speak up and wise to know our boundaries.

My husband and I walked our son into the school together. That may have been all he needed that day. It may have been all that we all needed in that season of our lives.

Is there an area you keep agreeing to that you need to speak up about? Doing something different may shift everything.

A couple of years before all this change occurred in our lives, if someone had told me we all would be going back to school, I would have said, "Okay, how will that work?" We serve the God of the impossible. He is looking for the willing and obedient.

> *"If you are willing and obedient, you shall eat the good of the land." Isaiah 1:19 (NKJV)*

Would you consider yourself in that category of willing and obedient? If not, why not? Do you think that it will work out for you any other way?

Moving Forward Journaling

_____

_____

_____

_____

_____

_____

_____

_____

_____

_____

_____

_____

_____

_____

_____

_____

_____

_____

_____

_____

_____

_____

_____

_____

CHAPTER 13

WILLING TO RECEIVE GIFTS FROM GOD

The week before my husband left to work out of town for a season was the week of the biggest snowstorm we had seen in a while. I got stuck in the snow while dropping off my little three-year-old at daycare. Thankfully, at the beginning of this school year, we were given an all-wheel drive minivan that was in amazing shape. This minivan replaced our twelve-passenger van, which was almost useless in the snow. God had so lovingly supplied this need and prompted this acquaintance to offer this vehicle to us at no charge.

Maneuvering through school traffic was so much easier in a smaller vehicle. It had heated seats, and a screen for watching DVDs was a blessing to our kids as well as us parents. It was clean and in great condition. It served us well for the season that I was driving seven kids to school. I wasn't crazy about becoming a "minivan mom," but I could overlook that for the few perks we were gaining without another car payment. I had driven the twelve-passenger van for fifteen years. God had showed Himself faithful once again. We still had the bigger van that we used to go places when my husband was along.

Before my husband left to go out of town, he insisted we get another vehicle—something that would do better in the snow. He was planning to leave the following week, and he said, "I'm getting you a different vehicle before I go."

I was sitting in my Bible school class when he told me this via text. I, on the other hand, wasn't feeling the same way. We had been in a huge financial hardship for a few years, and I didn't want another bill to deal with. My husband and I had sat through a lot of tense bill-paying sessions together where he was angry and overwhelmed with our financial situation, and I was speaking out verses on abundance and faith-filled words. (Go to the

Appendix for confessions concerning finances.) If his negativity about the lack of finances had continued, I would have had to leave the meeting. I would not, I could not, remain in that atmosphere.

I told the Lord, "I don't want another payment. I'm fine with the minivan. It will work out to drive this minivan longer." We had only had it for about five months. Then I said, "But if You want me to have it, I will take it." What I meant was that I would be willing to receive whatever He wanted to give me because I knew how good He was and that He always has my best in mind. I had already experienced His goodness in so many areas of my life. Why would I think I knew better in this area? I wasn't about to miss out on what God wanted me to have because I was afraid of an extra payment. I was not about to let fear stop me. Sometimes we resist what God wants to do. We get stuck in our limited mindsets, and we stay there. We stay in the same place financially, stay in the same old car, stay in the same job, and stay in the average or lukewarm spot because it's comfortable, but it doesn't take faith to stay there. The Word says, "It is impossible to please Him without faith."

What if we step out to the next place, and it takes God to make it happen? Shouldn't our daily life take faith? And if it doesn't, are we living big enough? Ask yourself where you are at. Are you living safe, comfortable, and easy when God is bidding you to let go of the physical securities and take a risk or step out on the water where there is nothing physical to hang on to? Stepping out on the water requires us to lean on, rely on, and keep our eyes on Jesus, the author and perfector of our faith.

"[looking away from all that will distract us and] focusing our eyes on Jesus, who is the Author and Perfecter of faith [the first incentive for our belief and the One who brings our faith to maturity], who for the joy [of accomplishing the goal] set before Him endured the cross, disregarding the shame, and sat down at the right hand of the throne of God [revealing His deity, His authority, and the completion of His work]." Hebrews 12:2

At this point, I knew I needed to yield to Him and His ways, even if they didn't make sense to me at the time. I've also learned and become aware that decisions don't need to make sense to me before I make them. Often, I just need to obey and step out in faith, knowing God is good. He is a rewarder of those who diligently seek Him.

"But without faith it is impossible to [walk with God and] please Him, for whoever comes [near] to God must [necessarily] believe that God exists and that He rewards those who [earnestly and diligently] seek Him." Hebrews 11:6

I had been diligently seeking Him, so I knew He wouldn't give me anything other than a reward. The next thing I knew, my husband wanted me to look at a new Suburban when I was done with class. With a yielded heart, I would go, trusting in the goodness of God and knowing He would work all things out for my good, simply because I love Him.

"And we know [with great confidence] that God [who is deeply concerned about us] causes all things to work together [as a plan] for good for those who love God, to those who are called according to His plan and purpose." Romans 8:28

I met him at the car lot after class to look at a 2019 Suburban. With tears running down my cheeks, we test-drove it. Comically, we realized this wasn't the one for us because my husband insisted that it needed heated seats, and this one happened not to have them. I'm not sure if he wanted to have heated seats more for himself or me, but the words "I want heated seats" kept coming out of his mouth.

I was still trying to wrap my head around the idea of getting a newer, different vehicle other than the express van or the minivan. I was having a hard time stopping the tears from streaming down my face. I wasn't upset or sad at all. I was overwhelmed with the thought that God would make this happen. I wasn't sure I had driven the minivan that was given to us long enough. I had nothing to say about having heated seats or not. All I had driven for years was the "commercially built" express van and ours didn't have any perks, only lots of seating and space. We finally decided the first one we looked at wasn't quite what we were looking for. Not only because it didn't have heated seats or leather seats but also because it was white instead of pearl white. It just didn't feel right.

We found our way to the next car lot. Right away, we spotted a pearl white Suburban that was a couple of years older, and the mileage was relatively low. As we looked at it, we saw that it had heated seats, not only in the front but also in the first back row of seats. It had a DVD player and not only one screen for the first back row of seats but another one for the second back row of seats. My husband and I agreed that we would step forward on this one. All the while, I was choked up and holding back tears.

The choked-up feeling and the tears were tears of thankfulness, knowing that God wanted this newer vehicle for us; otherwise, He would have stopped it. A couple of days later, after we were approved to get this vehicle, my husband asked me to go pick it up.

It was beautiful, and it was such an amazing gift from God to me. As I went to pick it up, I was holding back the tears again. As the salesman walked me through the vehicle, I was overwhelmed with the goodness and faithfulness of God. I continued to hold back the tears and tried to take in the information I was being given about this Suburban. The minute he was done and left me alone with it, I sobbed. I was in awe of my Heavenly Father, my Rock, my Redeemer, my Provider, Giver of MORE THAN I COULD ASK FOR OR IMAGINE …

I could barely see to get it started. Thankfully, we lived two minutes away from this car lot. I struggled to see the short distance home. The tears just kept coming. They wouldn't stop.

The snow continued to build up that following week when my husband left for his new job out of town. I was so thankful, realizing that if I had insisted on not having another payment, I would not have even made it out of our driveway. The snow was so deep. We live on the edge of town, so we have a gravel alleyway that only gets plowed if we hire someone to do it. We had sold the equipment to do it ourselves a few years prior.

Everything worked out financially. I could have stuck with the minivan, and God would have let me, but I would have missed out on seeing His faithfulness and love toward me. He loves us all. He sees and cares about every detail of our lives.

Are we willing to say yes to the extravagant gifts He wants to bless us with? Let's be more aware of what God wants for us rather than insisting on our own way.

Isn't God just so good? He does far over and above all we dare ask or think. What a gift to my children to have these DVD players and these heated seats. What a gift to me, a mom who had ten children and had driven an express twelve-passenger van for fifteen years without complaining. I continue to praise Him for revealing Himself as a gift giver and a rewarder. I give Him all the glory for what He has done.

Another testimony of receiving gifts from God is when my twelve-year-old son, Easton, and I rode down to Oklahoma with our oldest son, Luke, to bring him to college. First, we got a call from a random person who was associated with the Bible school our son would be attending. This person said he had found a note on his desk to call us. He was not sure where the note came from. He had been out of town for several days and returned home to find it. I had been asking God to supply a place for me to stay while I was down there. I was not going to be able to stay with my sons in the men's on-campus apartment. This man that called happened to know of a couple who opened their home to people visiting the Bible school. It was obvious that the Holy Spirit had prompted this connection for our trip that was just days away. I called the couple who were in their eighties and full of energy. They happened to have an open room. Our finances had been tight, so getting a hotel room would have been a stretch, but God made a way.

We enjoyed the ride down south. We watched God provide for our every need as the '79 Chevy kept acting up. We saw help come when we needed it. One time, we stalled in the middle of a busy intersection at 11:00 p.m. Some guys offered to help us push it to the side of the road while I called 911. I wanted to be sure help was on the way. We didn't know much about the area we were broken down in. We weren't sure what was nearby or how far the next town was.

As we waited, my son checked out the truck. He was fairly savvy with vehicle repairs, as he had redone this truck himself in his last couple of years of high school. A guy came up on his motorcycle and asked Luke a couple of questions about what was going on. He proceeded to work alongside my son until the problem was fixed in a half hour. As quickly as he came, he left. I'm certain he was an angel.

We were on our way again. Everything flowed smoothly for the final stretch of the trip. I stayed with the amazing, hospitable couple that the Lord had led me to. Easton and Luke bunked out at Luke's on-campus apartment. We enjoyed some visits and meals with the elderly couple I stayed with, and the wife offered to take us to the airport, which was an hour and a half away. We said our goodbyes to Luke. We prepared to leave the following day after getting Luke all settled in.

Earlier that spring, I had been offered some standby tickets if we were ever in need. We called this lady who had offered the tickets and were able to use them for the flights home. It was another way God provided for us during this trip. God continued to show Himself faithful.

We were dropped off at the airport, and my son and I quickly got all checked in and waited for our flight to depart. Flying standby is a whole other walk of faith. We wouldn't know until everyone was boarded whether there was room for one or both of us. I let the gal at the ticket counter know we were there so she could get us on the list. I was pretty sure standby was first come, first served. We sat down with a snack, believing God would open up seats for both of us.

All of a sudden, I said, "Easton, wouldn't it be cool if we got put in first class?" Not five minutes later, the gal from the counter walked over and said, "I put you both in first class!" Easton and I looked at each other with smirks on our faces. I turned to the ticket agent and said, "Awesome, thank you!" as if I had been expecting it.

We boarded the plane and found our seats in first class. I had never traveled that way before. We were given warm washcloths to wash before we ate. We were served an appetizer of warm nuts and a warm meal. We could have all the drinks we wanted, and we sat in the roomy, comfy seats. I was overjoyed, basking in the gift my son and I were given by God. What He will do for us if we believe!

Will you believe? He is good and a rewarder of those who trust in Him. As I was writing this book, I had to add this chapter. God wants us all to know just how generous He is! Just believe and be willing to receive whatever He has for you.

YOUR NEXT STEPS JOURNALING

_____

_____

_____

_____

_____

_____

_____

_____

_____

_____

_____

_____

_____

_____

_____

_____

_____

_____

_____

_____

_____

_____

_____

_____

_____

CHAPTER 14

Become a Covenant Life Coach?

I was in my second year of Bible school, my husband was working out of town, my children were continuing another year of public school and getting used to all the changes, and my life felt very hard. I was clinging to God with every step.

The Lord gave me a vision during that time. I was on a dock that was unstable. You know, the kind of dock that floats on the water and moves with each wave. I was getting used to the rocking, learning not to be moved by it. I realized that I no longer had anything physical to hold on to. There was nothing in my life physically that I could rely on, trust, or put my security in. What if this feeling of instability became normal? It was beginning to feel more normal the longer I kept standing through the thick and the thin.

I realized He was bidding me to take the next step, and it would be stepping off the dock that was already unstable and stepping out onto the water. Yes, like Peter was called to come out on the water with Jesus. There would be nothing physical to hang on to or even stand on as he stepped off the boat, but if he kept his eyes on Jesus, he would not sink.

> *"He said, 'Come!' So, Peter got out of the boat, and walked on the water and came toward Jesus." Matthew 14:29*

It was the same idea for me. Keeping my eyes on Jesus, the author and perfector of my faith, I would stay afloat and walk on water. I would be standing on Jesus, my Rock and my Salvation. He is my Rock, and "all other ground is sinking sand."

> *"'So everyone who hears these words of Mine and acts on them, will be like a wise man [a far-sighted, practical, and sensible man] who built his house on the rock. And the rain fell, and the floods and torrents came, and the winds blew and slammed against that house; yet it did not fall,*

because it had been founded on the rock. And everyone who hears these words of Mine and does not do them, will be like a foolish (stupid) man who built his house on the sand. And the rain fell, and the floods and torrents came, and the winds blew and slammed against that house; and it fell — and great and complete was its fall.'" Matthew 7:24–27

He is my "firm foundation," and I will not be shaken.

"He only is my rock and my salvation; My fortress and my defense, I will not be shaken or discouraged." Psalm 62:6

I was willing to step out, but I didn't know what I was stepping out onto yet. I knew He would be with me. I finished Bible school just as COVID-19 hit in March 2020. I had been asking the Lord prior to that what He wanted me to do next. I hadn't gotten any direction up to that point.

My seven children came home due to schools shutting down, and my husband was still on the road. I thought, *I guess I am homeschooling again.* I settled into that thought for the time being. I knew the Lord would give further direction when it was time. I would choose to just do the next thing, put another load of laundry in, make the next meal, and help my children with their schooling. I would choose to be content but not satisfied in that spot.

Our first grandbaby was born during that first week of the pandemic shutdown. We took a trip up to meet her. I'm thankful for the Lord's timing. We got to go enjoy our daughter's first baby and support them after a long labor and delivery. We were some of the only family members who were willing to travel at the time. We felt blessed to be able to do that. I know how fun it can be to show off your first baby.

One afternoon at the end of March, my fifteen-year-old daughter was on social media and said, "Mom, have you heard of this lady?" I hadn't. It was a mom coach. With her being a mom of seven children, my ears perked up. Large families were few and far between where we lived. I was interested in listening to her and what she had to say. I quickly found out that she had started a program for moms with recorded coaching for all areas of life. I bought the program for $97 per month. I started listening to coaching on finances. We had struggled with money, especially in the last several years, and I was interested in more biblical teaching on the subject.

In mid-May, I learned that she also offered a faith-based life coaching academy. I started watching interviews of other women who had become coaches, and I decided this type of work sounded interesting for my next step. I paid the refundable fee of $1,500 to have an interview with her to see if this would be a fit for me.

The interview went well. She said she would save a spot for me and encouraged me to read the information packet that I had missed reading prior to the interview. I agreed.

As I read through the information, I realized that the program would cost over $10K. Right away, I thought, "I can't do that. God, I'll work at Walmart, I'll work in the school system, I'll continue to hold Bible studies and reach people that way. I don't have to take this course." I pulled out the refundable money and continued to pursue what God would have me do.

It was getting close to summer break, and usually, I could picture what I would be doing during the summer. For some reason, I could not picture what I would be doing this particular summer. During previous summers, I spent time sitting at our local pool while the children swam. I would enjoy talking with other moms who were there. For some reason, I couldn't picture myself only doing that this summer.

As I sought the Lord for about a week and a half, I had no direction, and I felt confused and like all my vision for my future was gone. There was no specific spot for me at our church. Nothing else was appealing to me at all. I was willing to do anything, but nothing I was considering was creating any excitement.

I had walked with God long enough to know His voice and recognize when He was speaking to me. *What was wrong? Why was I feeling this way?* I took a step back toward life coaching, and I listened to one more interview. That was all it took.

I told my husband, "I *have* to do this. I know it seems like a lot of money, but I *have* to do this." It felt like I had a choice at that moment to obey money or God, and in my life, I had made following God my only option.

Will we put our treasure where our heart is?

> *"For where your treasure is, there your heart [your wishes, your desires, that on which your life centers] will be also."*
> *Matthew 6:21*

For a long time, we had focused on getting out of debt. Is that really the focus God wanted us to have?

Consider 2 Kings 4 and the story about Elisha and the woman's oil. I will summarize this story for you. The woman cried out to Elisha, saying that her dead husband's creditors were coming to take her boys as slaves. She was going to the man of God, possibly expecting an offering. He did not give her an offering; instead, he asked her what she had in her house. She replied that she had nothing except a little oil. He told her to go and *borrow* jars. Then go inside and shut the door; in other words, do this privately. Pour oil into all the jars until they are full, then the oil will stop flowing. Once the jars were full, Elisha told her to go, sell the oil, and pay her debts, and then the woman and her sons could live on what was left.

Check it out for yourself. It looks as though he told her to start a business. It would be worthwhile for you to look into what the Bible says about money and business.

Will you be willing to stop playing it safe? You don't need faith to live safe. Will you do the thing that makes you feel sick to your stomach, or will you choose to stay comfortable?

"But small is the gate and narrow and difficult to travel is the path that leads the way to [everlasting] life, and there are few who find it." Matthew 7:14

This narrow road will not be popular; the crowd will not be there. You may be traveling it alone, at least for a season. It will be difficult. You will be doing activities that are uncomfortable. That is why few find it or choose it.

In my story, we pulled out a credit card and put the full amount on it. I began attending this life coaching academy on June 1, 2020. Obeying God had become the only option in my life. I *had* to do this. I was uncomfortable and sick to my stomach but certain God was with me and us.

Before I started the training, I had become very free in life; I was living without regrets, I was watching what was coming out of my mouth, I was not being moved by circumstances, and I was living loved and loving others.

The previous fall, I remember meeting with several women one on one and doing individual Bible studies with them to help them move forward from whatever they were going through. I asked the Lord to show me how I could help them more. I believe this was the answer to the question I had asked Him—become a Covenant Life Coach.

What the training in this academy did for me was give me the tools of coaching to help other people. The training also stretched me to speak up in a group and opened me up to what could be possible for me. It started me on a path of walking out my purpose. One of those dreams was to write this book.

Directly after I finished the coaching academy in August 2020, I jumped into an inner circle for life and business coaching. I knew I needed more coaching and connection with like-minded people. I knew I needed to step into this and put money toward wisdom and spiritual growth. The cost of the inner circle was over $15K. Instead of thinking about the cost of something, it's important to focus on the value it holds for you and what God is asking you to do. This step has held so much value in my life. It got me started on growing my coaching business, building my platform on social media, writing my book, and starting a podcast … and this was just what I did.

We (my husband and I) finished our second year of the life and business coaching group. As this year of the inner circle was opening up, I told the Lord, "If you want me to join this again, you are going to have to provide." This same month, we would be closing on our third property and needed over $25K for that. I knew the Lord's plan for us would succeed, no matter what—whether we were in this coaching group again or not. He specifically supplied all that we needed to close on our property and to join the group again.

I coached my husband before I even finished the academy. He was not enjoying his job, so he quit his comfortable, safe home office job with the oil company to do what was on his heart. He took the step to start D12 of Montana Maintenance Co. It would have been easy for him to just stay put in his comfortable job because the insurance and pay were good.

We quickly realized that for us just to stay comfortable was not an option. After all, we have people to reach and an assignment to do in the Kingdom of God. We are ambassadors in chains, slaves of righteousness, and citizens of heaven.

> *"And pray for me, that words may be given to me when I open my mouth, to proclaim boldly the mystery of the good news [of salvation], for which I am an ambassador in*

chains. And pray that in proclaiming it I may speak boldly and courageously, as I should." Ephesians 6:19-20

"And having been set free from sin, you have become the slaves of righteousness [of conformity to God's will and purpose]." Romans 6:18

"But [we are different, because] our citizenship is in heaven. And from there we eagerly await [the coming of] the Savior, the Lord Jesus Christ." Philippians 3:20

We are called as children of God to serve Him and to help build His Kingdom on this earth. The Kingdom of God is, first of all, about yielding ourselves to the High King of Heaven. Then ruling over our assignment as kings and queens on this earth under Him. Finally, we are to serve others with the assignment He has given us.

"But first and most importantly seek (aim at, strive after) His kingdom and His righteousness [his way of doing and being right—the attitude and character of God], and all these things will be given to you also." Matthew 6:33

We purchased four multi-family properties in fourteen months. That same year, we started our maintenance company, and I started coaching. This was part of our assignment to take steps of faith to do what made us sick to our stomachs. We had inner peace and direction from the Lord to do it, but it has taken faith to walk it out. Was it easy? No! Every step was uncomfortable. I remember getting on one of our inner circle office hours calls and feeling so uncomfortable. I said, "I am feeling super uncomfortable right now." Every ounce of my body was crawling; I was so uncomfortable. Guess what? I am still alive; I didn't die.

Remember the vision God gave me about stepping out on the water with nothing but Him to cling to? This season of our lives was what He was preparing me for with that vision.

As we took each step from becoming a Covenant Life Coach to starting the maintenance company to buying those few properties, nothing made sense. But it was all working. That's exactly where we needed to be. We've kept our eyes on Jesus, the author and finisher of our faith, our Lord, our Master … Let me just get this verse out here:

> "[Looking away from all that will distract us and] focusing our eyes on Jesus, who is the Author and Perfecter of faith [the first incentive for our belief and the One who

brings our faith to maturity], who for the joy [of accomplishing the goal] set before Him endured the cross, disregarding the shame, and sat down at the right hand of the throne of God [revealing His deity, his authority, and the completion of His work]." Hebrews 12:2

The question is: Will you endure until the end; will you take the narrow path; will you throw off the weights that are entangling you?

"Therefore, since we are surrounded by so great a cloud of witnesses [who by faith have testified to the truth of God's absolute faithfulness], stripping off every unnecessary weight and the sin which so easily and cleverly entangles us, let us run with endurance and active persistence the race that is set before us." Hebrews 12:1

Will you forget the past so you can reach toward the goal of the high call of God?

"Brothers and sisters, I do not consider that I have made it my own yet; but one thing I do: forgetting what lies behind and reaching forward to what lies ahead, I press on toward the goal to win the [heavenly] prize of the upward call of God in Christ Jesus." Philippians 3:13–14

Friend, we have a race to run and a call to answer. Will you show yourself worthy?

Many are called, but few are chosen, which means literally few choose to accept the invitation and obey the conditions of the call. They may feel it's too hard; they may feel they are too busy. But can I ask you what you are too busy doing? The Word tells us that those who are willing to lose their life will find it.

> *"Whoever finds his life [in this world] will [eventually] lose it [through death], and whoever loses his life [in this world] for My sake will find it [that is, life with Me for all eternity]." Matthew 10:39*

We have been bought with a price; therefore, honor God with your body.

> *"You were bought with a price [you were actually purchased with the precious blood of Jesus and made His own]. So then, honor and glorify God with your body." 1 Corinthians 6:20*

What are you waiting for, Church? We can't stay here. We've got a charge to keep. We have a God to serve. We've got sick people to heal. We've got a gospel to preach. We've got broken hearts to bind ... Move,

Church. Move, Church … We are not waiting on a move of God; WE ARE A MOVE OF GOD. (Elevation Worship)

What is God calling you to do? Consider working with someone, even me, a Covenant Life Coach, and take a step toward renewing your mind, a step toward wisdom and spiritual growth. You only live once, so walk into your purpose; you don't want to miss it by staying comfortable.

Moving Forward Journaling

_____

_____

_____

_____

_____

_____

_____

_____

_____

_____

_____

_____

_____

_____

_____

_____

_____

_____

_____

_____

_____

_____

CONCLUSION

Wow, thank you for taking this journey with me. Maybe you are starting your walk of faith, maybe you are continuing your walk of faith, and maybe you are ready to take your life of faith to the next level.

Wherever you are in your journey, I encourage you to step it up a notch. If you aren't a believer yet, start that relationship with Him today. Reach out to Him and tell Him you want Him to be Lord over your life and thank Him for forgiving your sins. Then start reading your Bible, believing it, and obeying it. Start talking to God. Make sure you take time to listen to what He is saying to you. He will speak to your heart. You are led by His Spirit, friend.

If you are a believer and haven't really been living like one, start believing God in at least one area of your life—that spot where you are worrying and afraid of what could happen instead of believing that it will work out for your good because you love God. Since you call yourself a believer, start acting like one. Start believing Him. Start believing the Word of God over the facts of your circumstances.

If you have been walking by faith, continue, but start believing God for bigger things and start taking bigger, riskier steps. Those kinds of steps that make you sick to your stomach. Those dreams that are scary and can't happen without God. Start believing in the impossible in your life. Our faith walk pleases Him. He wants to show up big in your life and in this world. Start dreaming bigger.

So, what is your next step?

What weights do you need to throw off so you can run your race?

Remember, you are Covered! He's got you. What if you believed that? What could your life look like if you believed the Word over your circumstances?

What would it look like for you to start walking in the goodness and fullness of God?

What if you started believing in healing?

You could start using the name of Jesus when something happens. What if His name actually changes your circumstances?

What if you started thinking or believing something different? What if you believed you didn't have to be broke or live paycheck to paycheck?

What if what got you here won't get you there?

What if you have to think differently to get the results you want?

What if you let yourself dream again?

What could that make possible?

The Word of God says:

> *"As he thinks in his heart, so is he." Proverbs 23:7 (NKJV)*

> *"And do not be conformed to this world [any longer with its superficial values and customs], but be transformed and progressively changed [as you mature spiritually] by the renewing of your mind [focusing on godly values and ethical attitudes], so that you may prove [for yourselves] what the will of God is, that which is good and acceptable and perfect [in His plan and purpose for you]." Romans 12:2*

The idea of being Covered comes from the thought that those of us who are in Christ are Covered by His Name, the Name above all names.

> *"The name of the Lord is a strong tower; The righteous runs to it and is safe and set on high [far above evil]." Proverbs 18:10*

Being Covered also reflects the idea of Him being our fortress, the heavily protected building or the impenetrable place. He is our refuge, which is a safe place.

> *"I will say of the Lord, 'He is my refuge and my fortress, My God, in whom I trust [with great confidence, and on whom I rely]!'" Psalm 91:2*

Living Covered in His blood means we are cleansed of our sinful nature and made new in Christ.

"But if we [really]walk in the Light [that is, live each day and every day in conformity with the precepts of God], as He Himself is in the Light, we have [true, unbroken] fellowship with one another [He is with us, and we with Him], and the blood of Jesus His Son cleanses us from all sin [by erasing the stain of sin, keeping us cleansed from sin in all its forms and manifestations]." 1 John 1:7

Can you picture yourself Covered? Can you live Covered in every area? It does not matter what the circumstances are. He's got you surrounded by His love. You have been hidden in Christ.

"For you died [to this world], and your [new, real] life is hidden with Christ in God." Colossians 3:3

You can live in triumph while going through trials when you live Covered by Him.

"But thanks be to God, who always leads us in triumph in Christ, and through us spreads and makes evident everywhere the sweet fragrance of the knowledge of Him." 2 Corinthians 2:14

Take your time in answering the questions in this conclusion. Take your life to a whole other level. He's with you through it all.

Thank you for taking the time to read my story.

You have a story, too. Share it everywhere you go.

Love you, Friend,

Jackie Dighans

YOUR NEXT STEPS JOURNALING

_____

_____

_____

_____

_____

_____

_____

_____

_____

_____

_____

_____

_____

_____

_____

_____

_____

_____

_____

_____

_____

_____

_____

_____

APPENDIX

I Am a Wife Confession

July 2019 – Jackie Dighans – Covenant Life Coach

A wise, understanding,
and prudent (sensible, well advised, cautious, far-
sighted) wife is from the Lord. Proverbs 19:14

I am a fruitful vine in the heart
of our home. Psalm 128:3

The heart of my husband safely and confidently
trusts in me and relies on and believes in me securely,
so that he has no lack of honest gain or need of
dishonest spoil. Proverbs 31:11

I comfort, encourage, and do him only
good as long as I have life. Proverbs 31:12

I am an excellent wife, a crown (top or highest part) of
my husband. I perfect, complete, and put the finishing
touches on him as I walk in Christ. Proverbs 12:4

I am a good thing for my husband, and he obtains favor
from the Lord because he has found in me a true wife.
Proverbs 18:22

I see to it that I respect my husband – I notice him,
regard him, honor him, prefer him, appreciate him,
venerate or revere him, and esteem, value, prize and
favor him. I defer to him, am devoted to him, praise,
adore, enjoy, deeply love, and admire him exceedingly.
Ephesians 5:33, 1 Peter 3:2

My Amazing Husband Confession

August 2019 – Jackie Dighans – Covenant Life Coach

My husband loves me as Christ loved
the church and gave Himself for her.

He washes me with the Word.

He lives with me in an understanding way.

He nourishes and cherishes me
and loves me as his own body.

He has left his father and mother
and cleaves, is joined, and sticks to me, his wife.

We are one. Ephesians 5:22–33

My husband is a man/ruler of discernment,
understanding, and knowledge. He is stable.
Proverbs 28:2

My husband refreshes others,
and we, too, are refreshed.

He prospers because he is generous. Proverbs 11:25

My husband reverently and worshipfully fears the Lord and delights in His Word, therefore he is blessed.

My husband is known in the city's gates when he sits among the elders of the land. Proverbs 31:23

Dighans Family Confession

March 2017 – Jackie Dighans – Covenant Life Coach

We reverently and worshipfully fear God,
and it is the beginning of wisdom and skill.

We have the mind of Christ, and we can do all things
through Him who gives us strength.

Our work is committed to
the Lord, and our plans are established.

Because we obey the Lord, our possessions, and
everything we put our hands to, are blessed.

We have been lavished in God's love;
therefore, we love each other and others.

We have freedom of utterance. We open our mouths
with boldness and courage as we ought in both song
and speech, that we may proclaim the mystery of the
gospel for which we are ambassadors in chains.

We are joyful when we face trials and temptations
because we expect them to produce godliness in us.

We were made for signs and wonders, not destruction.

He is able to do exceedingly, abundantly above
all we can imagine according to the power
that is at work in us.

We are delivered from the wicked.

We are taught of the Lord and great is our peace.

We humble ourselves in the sight of the Lord,
and He lifts us up.

I Am a Virtuous Woman Confession

July 2019 – Jackie Dighans – Covenant Life Coach

I am a saintly, upstanding,
high-minded, virtuous woman.

I speak wisdom, seek wisdom,
walk in wisdom, and listen to wisdom.

I show honor, I am honorable,
and I win honor for my husband.

The joy of the Lord is my strength.

I rejoice in the truth. I rejoice in the Lord,
and I rejoice in the day.

Kindness is on my tongue.

I fear the Lord, and it is
the beginning of wisdom and skill.

I am noble, righteous, and good.

I am a provider, source,
and supplier of desirable qualities.

I am industrious, diligent, and hardworking.

I am blessed, and I, in turn, bless others. I am a blessing.

I walk in dignity and am worthy
of honor because of Christ in me.

He Is My Source Confession

July 2019 – Jackie Dighans – Covenant Life Coach

He deals bountifully with me (largely, fully, superabundantly). Psalm 119:17

He supplies all my needs according to His riches in glory. Philippians 4:19

God is able to make all grace abound toward me, that I, always having all sufficiency in all things, may have an abundance for every good work. 2 Corinthians 9:8

The Lord is my Shepherd [to feed, to guide, and to shield me], I shall not want. Psalm 23:1

I am debt-free by the miracle power of Jesus.

No more late fees.

No more overdraft fees.

He is my shield and my exceeding great reward. Genesis 15:1

COVERED

ABOUT THE AUTHOR

Jackie Dighans is a daughter of God Most High. She has been married to her husband, Justin, for twenty-nine years. Together, they have ten children (yes, they are all biological; no, there are not any twins). The children range from seven to twenty-six years old. They have three married children and three grandchildren. Six children are still in the home attending public school, and one is single, taking the next steps after graduating from high school. Jackie lives with her family in rural southeastern Montana. Jackie and Justin own properties and other businesses that they work as a family. Jackie was a homeschool mom for almost twenty years. She attended three years of Bible school and has a certificate in Biblical Studies. Jackie is a Covenant Life Coach. She enjoys speaking at women's events, conferences, retreats, and other services. Jackie helps people come in alignment with the Covenant of God so they can live the full lives He has planned for them. She helps people throw off the weights and sin that entangle them and forget the past so they can run their race and reach the goal of the high call of God.

Author's Services

As a Covenant Life Coach,
Jackie Dighans offers one-on-one and group coaching.

She is a public speaker.
She enjoys speaking at retreats, women's events,
conferences, and other services.

Contact her at jackiedighans@gmail.com.

You can also find her on Facebook, Instagram,
TikTok, and YouTube at Jackie Dighans.

Her podcast called Dripping with
Abundance is on Spotify.

Made in the USA
Monee, IL
02 August 2023

40319203R00127